God's Little Devotional Book
for Fathers

God's Little
Devotional Book
for Fathers

eagle

Guildford, Surrey

Copyright © Honor Books

Originally published by Honor Books, Oklahoma, USA. This edition published in 1998 in the UK by Eagle, an imprint of Inter Publishing Service (IPS) Ltd, PO Box 530, Guildford, Surrey GU2 5FN.

British Library Cataloguing in Publication Data. A catalogue record for this book is available from the British Library.

All rights reserved. No part of this publication may be reproduced or transmitted in any form or by any means, electronic or mechanical, including photocopying, recording or any information storage and retrieval system, without either prior permission in writing from the publisher or a licence permitting restricted copying.
In the United Kingdom such licences are issued by the Publishers Licensing Society Ltd, 90 Tottenham Court Road, London W1P 9HE.

Scripture quotations used in this book are as follows:
AMP – *Amplified Bible*
GNB – *Good News Bible*
KJV – *Authorised King James Version*
NAS – *New American Standard Bible* © The Lockman Foundation, 1960, 1962, 1963, 1968, 1971, 1973, 1975, 1977
NIV – *New International Version* © Hodder & Stoughton
NKJ – *New King James* © Thomas Nelson
RSV – *Revised Standard Version* © Division of Christian Education of the National Council of the Churches of Christ in the USA
TLB – *The Living Bible* © Tyndale House, 1971

Printed in the UK by Cox & Wyman Ltd, Reading, Berks.
ISBN No: 0 86347 324 5

Acknowledgments

We acknowledge and thank the following people for the quotes used in this book: Billy Graham (12), T. DeWitt Talmadge (14), Josh McDowell (18), James Dobson (20,26,94,132,174,184,190,248), Glen Wheeler (22), Paul Lewis (24), Larry Christenson (28), General Douglas MacArthur (32,98), Dr. Anthony P. Witham (34), Elbert Hubbard (36), Robert Schuller (38), David Jeremiah (40), Tim Hansel (42,216), Eleanor Roosevelt (46), Sydney Harris (48), Abraham Lincoln (50), A.W. Tozer (54), Anthony Evans (56), Dwight L. Moody (60,76,142,242), David Shibley (62), Henry Ward Beecher (64,200,230), Martin Luther King, Jr. (68), Mark Twain (70,304), M. Scott Peck (72), Bill Cosby (74,286), Robert Green Ingersoll (78), Terence (82), Josh Billings (84), Victor Borge (86), John E. Anderson (88), Dennis Rainey (92), Susannah Wesley (96), Caroline Fry (100), Gordon MacDonald (104,110,234), William Langland (106), Henry Home (Lord Kames) (108), Thomas Jefferson (112), Mike Murdock (114), Don Marquis (116), Paul Tillich (118), John Locke (120,250), Calvin Coolidge (122), Frank Crane (124), R. Kent Hughes (126), Cecil G. Osborne (128), Wilhelm Busch (130), David Schwartz (134), C.H. Spurgeon (138), John R. Throop (144), James Oliver (148), Anne Bradstreet (150), Alan Beck (152), Ross Campbell (154), Peter DeVries (156), H.E. Jansen (160), Mencius (164), V. Gilbert Beers (166), Tagore (168), Kathryn McCarthy Graham (170), Hugh Prather (176),

Friedrich Wilheim Nietzsche (178), Albert Einstein (180), Nancy Samalin (186), Helen Andelin (188), Herbert Hoover (192), Robert South (196), Margaret Fuller (198), John Wooden (202), Aristotle (204), Stafano Guazzo (206), Harold A. Hulbert (208), W. Cecil (210), Gary Smalley and Paul Trent (218), Henry Van Dyke (220), James Openheim (222), Dr. Ronald Levant and John Kelly (224), Margaret Thatcher (232), Doris Mortman (236), Richard Exley (240), Dr. J. Kuriansky (244), Gigi Graham Tchividjian (246), Monta Crane (274), Lion (276), Guy Lombardo (280), Robert C. Savage (282), Lord Rochester (284), Benjamin Franklin (288), Lewis B. Hershey (292), Helen Rowland (294), Oliver Wendell Holmes (298), John Gratton (302,310), Paul Harvey (306,312), and H.V. Prochnow (308).

Introduction

Virtually every father knows what a 'good dad' should do and be. Equally so, virtually every person can use an occasional reminder of what it is he knows to be good, just and true. *God's Little Devotional Book for Fathers* serves as such a reminder.

In this book, you'll find short, to-the-point illustrations and stories that sometimes explain, sometimes amuse and sometimes hit hard. They are linked to quotations – both familiar and new – and to passages of Scripture, so that each devotional provides a message that is both timely and timeless. In many cases, you'll find these devotionals provide excellent anecdotes to share with your children. And on those occasions in which you are asked to lead a devotional time – perhaps for an organization to which you or one of your children belong – you'll find this book a ready reference for sharing a brief message that is meaningful and memorable.

The Word of God gives us the principle for acquiring God's truth in our lives: 'For precept must be upon precept, precept upon precept; line upon line, line upon line; here a little, and there a little' (Isaiah 28:10). *God's little Devotional Book for Fathers is* guaranteed to provide insight and inspiration to fathers everywhere!

There are many ways
to measure success;
not the least of which
is the way your child
describes you when
talking to a friend.

A child's glory is his father.
Proverbs 17:6b (TLB)

Two little boys were discussing their lives one day including the various behavioural patterns of their parents. One boy finally asked, 'Does your Daddy sit in the den a lot after he comes home from work?'

'No,' his friend replied, 'he growls all over the place at our house.'

Your children not only have a candid opinion about you, but they are also likely to copy your behaviour, both good and bad. Even if your child doesn't particularly like what you do – when asked objectively about it – he or she is likely to behave in the same way unconsciously A two-year-old might walk with a swagger . . . just like Dad. A three-year-old is likely to use all the words his parents use, even the ones inappropriate for polite company! Above all, children imitate the way their parents behave one to the other.

Three little girls were playing house one day taking turns playing various roles, when one of them said to another, 'Now you be the daddy.' The little girl pouted for a minute and then said, 'I don't want to be the daddy. I want to talk, and besides, what would I use for a remote control?'

Listen to your children. You may hear an echo!

A young successful attorney said: 'The greatest gift I ever received was a gift I got one Christmas when my dad gave me a small box. Inside was a note saying, "Son, this year I will give you 365 hours, an hour every day after dinner." My dad not only kept his promise,' he said, 'but every year he renewed it and it was the greatest gift I ever had in my life. I am the result of his time.'

Therefore be careful how you walk, not as unwise men but as wise, making the most of your time . . .
Ephesians 5:15,16 (NAS)

Young Tom attended the best schools Augusta offered, but he always considered his real instructor to be his father. Long before the age when most boys are studying, young Tom was receiving from his father an education that was highly varied, extremely practical and exceptionally sound academically.

Father and son were near-constant companions, but Sunday afternoons were especially devoted to young Tom's training. While Tom sat on the floor or leaned against an inverted chair, his father – a parson by profession – would pour into Tom's spellbound ears the tales of his own experience, learning and thought. Tom's father was a man of in-depth information on the affairs of the world, literature and theology. He coupled a robust imagination with an ability to reason clearly and focus on facts.

Tom eventually earned a doctorate of his own and became president of Princeton University. He also was elected governor of New Jersey. By the time he was elected President of the United States and became the foremost architect of the League of Nations, he had dropped entirely the use of his first name, Thomas. We know him in history simply as Woodrow Wilson – perhaps the most highly educated president in the history of our nation.

You don't need to show your child the world in order to be a great father. You only need to show him the best of *your* world.

How to curb juvenile
delinquency: 1. Take time
with your children.
2. Set your children a good
example. 3. Give your children
ideals for living. 4. Have a lot
of activities planned.
5. Discipline your children.
6. Teach them about God.

*. . . but be thou an example of the
believers, in word, in conversation, in
charity, in spirit, in faith, in purity.*
1 Timothy 4:12 (KJV)

*Train up a child in the way he should go:
and when he is old, he will not
depart from it.*
Proverbs 22:6 (KJV)

Many a parent has moaned with regard to their children who are young adults and away from home: 'I did everything I knew to do to be a good parent, and it looks as if nothing has worked.' In fact, the good seeds that the parents have sown are still planted deep in the soil of the child's life. It's at this point that the parent must turn to the only thing he or she *can* do effectively: pray!

Pray daily. Pray persistently. Pray specifically. And above all, pray with faith that God not only hears, but will answer.

A man once said to his friend, 'I believe if you thought the Lord told you to jump through a stone wall, you'd jump.' The friend replied, 'If the Lord told me to jump through a wall, it would be my business to jump, and it would be His business to make a hole.'

The same goes for parenting. The Lord tells us to do our part – to raise our children up according to His commandments and to the best of the knowledge we have – and then we must trust Him to do His part in our children's lives.

You can sow, but only God can grow. Trust Him to do that work in your child's life today – to bring to life that which is lying dormant and to cause your child to grow and flourish into the fullness of the stature of Christ Jesus!

'Do you remember your father?' asked the judge sternly, 'that father whom you have disgraced?' The prisoner answered: 'I remember him perfectly. When I went to him for advice or companionship, he would look up from his book on the Law of Trusts, and say, "Run away boy I am busy." My father finished his book and here I am.'

Fathers, do not exasperate your children; instead, bring them up in the training and instruction of the Lord.
Ephesians 6:4 (NIV)

Albert's father, one of the busiest architects in Mannheim, regarded architecture as merely a means to a financial end. He told a visitor: 'It made no difference to me what I did. My main concern was to make money.' His money gave young Albert all the material privileges a young boy might imagine: a fourteen-room apartment, servants, a chauffeur, a nanny. Young Albert, however, received neither affection nor understanding from his parents.

Little Albert felt lonely in the family of five. When he began public high school in Heidelberg, two of his new friends quickly encouraged him into mischief. Albert's heart swelled with pride whenever his name was entered in the classbook because of some prank he had pulled, and he punctiliously noted the event in his own diary.

At age 18, despite a brilliance in and love for mathematics, Albert decided to follow his father's advice and study architecture, no doubt hoping to 'earn' his father's love in this way. Ten years later, his study was richly rewarded when he gained the unrestricted affection of someone who became a 'surrogate' father figure to him: the Führer and Chancellor of the German Reich.

It was not only in architecture that Albert Speer earned Hitler's regard. He became Hitler's Minister of Armaments and War Production, a job in which he had only one goal in mind: to earn 'marks' in history's book.

The way each day
will look to you all
starts with *who*
you're looking to.

I lift up my eyes to the hills –
where does my help come from?
My help comes from the LORD,
the Maker of heaven and earth.
Psalm 121:1,2 (NIV)

A young man was learning to plough with a tractor. He climbed onto the seat of the tractor for his first 'solo run', pulled the lever that dropped the plough to the ground, and started across the field. After he had gone a few yards, he turned around to look at the furrow he was making. He became entranced by the rushing flow of topsoil along the ploughshare – the rich, black soil turning over in a seemingly endless ribbon. By the time he turned back to see where he was going, he realized that the wheel of the tractor had swerved a number of times. Glancing again behind him, he saw a wavering furrow, a permanent etching into the earth of his wandering eye.

The secret to pulling a straight furrow is not in watching the furrow as it is made, but to set one's sights across the field at a distant point, and to keep the nose of the tractor moving squarely towards that point. The point on which the eyes are fixed must be a fixed point, such as a tree, barn or hilltop. Only the *occasional* brief backward glance is allowable!

The same holds true for our life of faith. We are to keep our eyes fixed upon Jesus, who never changes, and to line up our behaviour with His Word, looking back only rarely on our ministry and outreach efforts.

Every day you make choices of how you will spend your time and on what you will focus. Be sure you focus on building a relationship with your child.

The greatest thing a father
can do for his children
is to love their mother.

*So husbands ought to love their own
wives as their own bodies; he who
loves his wife loves himself.*
Ephesians 5:28 (NKJ)

A teaching that has resurfaced frequently in the history of the Christian Church is this:

- A child deduces his basic concept of God based upon the image of his own father – the human father is seen as a reflection of the Heavenly Father.
- A child draws his basic concept of the Church based upon the example of his own mother – her daily practical nurturing, teaching, admonishing and disciplining are internalized by the child as a reflection of these same spiritual qualities provided by the Church.
- A child draws his understanding of how God relates to the Church – and thus, how God relates to him as a member of the Church – by watching how his father relates to his mother, and she to him.

Your example of how you treat your wife is a living parable to your children about how God wants to relate to them! Are you available to your wife? Do you praise and support her? Are you helpful to her? Do you provide for her?

Ask yourself today, 'Do I treat my wife as I hope the Lord will treat me?'

If you want your child to accept your values when he reaches his teen years, then you must be worthy of his respect during his younger days.

. . . a model for you, so that you would follow our example.
2 Thessalonians 3:9 (NAS)

Louisa May Alcott not only accepted her parents' values . . . but perpetuated them! She grew up in an extremely generous home even though life was bare in their house, which didn't even have a stove. A friend once observed that their extremely plain and meagre meals were often reduced from three a day to two if there was a family who might be in need. The Alcotts themselves, however, would have been the last to consider themselves poor or feel sorry for themselves.

Louisa was once invited to visit, by herself, in Providence. With no other children in the house, she became bored after a few days. She found some dirty, ragged children who seemed to her ideal playmates and she played with them for a long time in the barn. Finding them poorly fed and hungry, she ran in haste to the pantry, which was unguarded at the time, and helped herself to figs and cakes for all. When her hostess discovered what she had done, she scolded her soundly and sent her to the attic to ponder her outrageous behaviour. Dear Louisa. She didn't have the faintest idea that 'feeding the poor' was wrong. She was later found not crying or the least bit repentant, but rather, angry that her hostess had not also offered more for her to take to her new friends!

A child is not likely
to find a father in
God unless he finds
something of God
in his father.

*And you should follow my example,
just as I follow Christ's.*
1 Corinthians 11:1 (TLB)

Jim, a church elder, was assigned to oversee the evangelism of a group of Vietnamese refugees who had just moved into the church's neighbourhood. He felt especially drawn to Sun Lee and his family who had no possessions, knew no one and needed help in every way. Jim began by helping the family get food and then he helped Sun Lee find a job.

Jim wanted so much to tell Sun Lee about Jesus Christ, but since he didn't speak Vietnamese and the refugees knew very little English, he found it difficult to communicate. Both Jim and Sun Lee began to learn as much of each other's language as possible so they could become better friends.

One day Jim felt that he finally knew enough Vietnamese to tell Sun Lee about Jesus, but the more he talked, the more confused Sun Lee seemed to be. Finally Sun Lee blurted out, 'Is your God like you?'

Jim replied, 'Oh, He's far, far greater.'

Sun Lee interrupted, 'If He's like you, Jim, I want to know Him.'

The most effective communication is the 'word' of your deeds.

A father's words are like
a thermostat that sets the
temperature in the house.

The tongue has the power of life and
death, and those who love
it will eat its fruit.
Proverbs 18:21 (NIV)

We've all no doubt heard the popular phrase, 'You're talking so loud I can't hear you.' An old poem confirms that good advice about 'taming the tongue' has been offered by virtually every culture, tribe and race!

'The boneless tongue, so small and weak,
Can crush and kill,' declares the Greek.
'The tongue destroys a greater horde,'
The Turk asserts, 'than does the sword.'
The Persian proverb wisely saith,
'A lengthy tongue – an early death!'
Or sometimes takes this form instead,
'Don't let your tongue cut off your head.'
'The tongue can speak a word whose speed,'
Say the Chinese, 'outstrips the steed.'
The Arab sages said in part,
'The tongue's great storehouse is the heart.'
From Hebrew was the maxim sprung,
'Thy feet should slip, but ne'er the tongue.'
The sacred writer crowns the whole,
'Who keeps the tongue doth keep his soul.'

The solution to the arms race . . . rising rates of crime, abuse and divorce . . . may very well lie . . . in the tongue.

While I don't
minimize the vital
role played by a mother,
I believe a successful
family begins with
her husband.

*He must be one who manages his own
household well, keeping his children
under control with all dignity.*
1 Timothy 3:4 (NAS)

In their classic book *Cheaper by the Dozen*, Frank B. Gilbreth, Jr., and Ernestine Gilbreth Carey describe their father as a man who 'always practised what he preached, and it was just about impossible to tell where his scientific management company ended and his family life began. His office was always full of children, and he often took two or three of us, and sometimes all twelve, on business trips . . .

'On the other hand, our house at Montclair, New Jersey was a sort of school for scientific management and the elimination of wasted motions.'

Gilbreth installed work charts in the bathrooms, took moving pictures of his children doing chores to help identify wasted motion, and insisted that a child who wanted extra pocket money submit a sealed bid, with the lowest bidder getting the contract. Still, his children didn't seem to mind their regimented life. Why? Primarily because Dad 'had a respect for them, too, and didn't mind showing it'. He believed about children that 'there's no limit to what you can teach. Really it was a love of children more than anything else that made him want a pack of his own.'

It's not the rules that a father exacts that cause a child to rebel, but rather, a lack of love and respect.

Happy is the child who happens in upon his parent from time to time to see him on his knees . . . or going aside regularly to keep times with the Lord.

*Let the heart of them rejoice
that seek the LORD.
Seek the LORD, and his strength:
seek his face evermore.*
Psalm 105:3,4 (KJV)

'You must have a good heart,' one man said to his child, "if you are going to act right in this world.' And then in illustrating his point he continued, 'Suppose my watch was not keeping time very well. Would it do any good if I went to the town clock and made the hands of my watch point exactly the same as those of the larger clock in the square? No, of course not! Soon my watch would be just as inaccurate as before. Rather, I should take my watch to a watchmaker, or to a jewellery shop that repairs watches. It is only when my watch has been cleaned and repaired that its hands will be able to keep time accurately all day long.'

When we spend time in prayer, we are, in like manner, going to the Heart Maker, asking Him to 'clean and repair our hearts' from the damage caused by sins we have committed. We are asking Him to put us right again on the inside, so that we can more clearly discern right from wrong. When our children see us doing this, they are much more likely to go to the Heart Maker when they feel their own lives in disarray or 'out of sync' – rather than turn to the world and reset their souls according to its standards and priorities.

When God measures
a man, He puts the
tape around the
heart instead
of the head.

*'The LORD does not look at the things
man looks at. Man looks at the
outward appearance, but the
LORD looks at the heart.'*
1 Samuel 16:7 (NIV)

As he was returning home from the Capitol one evening, Senator John Stennis was robbed at gunpoint. Even though Stennis turned over what little of value he was carrying, the robbers shot him twice, hitting him in the stomach and leg. The surgeons at Walter Reed Medical Center laboured for more than six hours to repair the damage and save his life.

Also on his way home that evening was Senator Mark Hatfield, who had clashed often and sharply with Stennis. The two were at virtually opposite ends of the political spectrum. However, when Hatfield heard on his car radio what had happened, he immediately drove to the hospital. There, he quickly discerned that the switchboard staff were overwhelmed with the many incoming calls from Stennis' fellow senators, reporters and friends. He said to an operator, '1 know how to work one of these; let me help you out.' He helped answer phones until daylight when the calls subsided. Then, without fanfare, he quietly introduced himself as he was leaving, 'My name is Hatfield . . . happy to help out on behalf of a man I deeply respect.'

'Bigness' means being free of pettiness, grudges, vengeance and prejudice. It means caring unconditionally, helping unassumingly.

O Lord . . . build me a
son whose heart will be
clear, whose goal will
be high, a son who will
master himself before
he seeks to master other
men; one who will
reach into the future,
yet never forget the past.

A wise son brings joy to his father . . .
Proverbs 10:1 (NIV)

Thomas. Watson, Jr., writes in *Father, Son & Co. – My Life at IBM and Beyond* about his first days as CEO: 'When my father died in 1956 – six weeks after making me head of IBM – I was the most frightened man in America. For ten years he had groomed me to succeed him, and I had been the young man in a hurry, eager to take over, cocky and impatient. Now, suddenly I had the job – but what I didn't have was Dad there to back me up.'

Watson admits that he 'didn't have much motivation as a youth'. He was neither student nor athlete. At Brown University, he spent so much time flying airplanes that he barely graduated. His father encouraged him, however, saying, 'At some point, something will catch hold and you are going to be a great man.' After World War II, Watson returned home 'confident, for the first time, that I might be capable of running IBM'. And he did! During his 15 years as head of IBM, the company entered the computer era and grew more than tenfold, becoming a $7.5 billion-a-year business. He says of the success, '1 think I was at least successful enough that people could say I was the worthy son of a worthy father.'

Too much love never
spoils children.
Children become spoiled
when we substitute
'presents' for 'presence'.

We loved you dearly – so dearly that we
gave you not only God's message,
but our own lives too.
1 Thessalonians 2:8 (TLB)

A man once gave his little boy a baseball and a baseball bat . . . but he never pitched the ball to his son or showed him how to swing the bat. He gave his boy a toy gun . . . but he never showed him how to play 'cop' with it, instead of robber.

A man once gave his son a pocketknife . . . but he never showed him how to use it to carve an animal from a bar of soap. He gave his boy a BB-gun . . . but he never took him to a firing range to show him how to use it safely or along on his hunting trips.

The man was astonished the day two policemen came to his door with a tale about his boy and others in the neighbourhood who had formed a malicious gang. 'Not my son,' he said. 'I've never taught him violence.'

'Perhaps not,' the policeman answered. 'But in the shed that the boys were using for their headquarters, we found clubs, guns and knives.'

'Perhaps,' the other policeman added, 'you didn't teach your son how *not* to be violent.'

Never expect your child to understand the world from the things you give to him. He needs you to show him what to expect in life, how to embrace life and to live life to its fullest.

Live truth instead of professing it.

But be doers of the word, and not hearers only, deceiving yourselves.
James 1:22 (NKJ)

A reporter once asked Sam Rayburn, who was Speaker of the House of Representatives at the time:

'Mr. Speaker, you see at least a hundred people a day. You tell each one yes or no. You never seem to make notes on what you have told them, but I have never heard of your forgetting anything you have promised them. What is your secret?'

Rayburn's eyes flashed as he answered, 'If you tell the truth the first time, you don't have to remember.'

Truth extends to honesty. If you are honest in all of your dealings, you never have to remember whom you may have cheated.

Truth extends to positive encouragement. If you speak a good truth of all people, you never have to avoid anybody.

Truth spills over into the 'implied'. If you refuse to give false impressions, you never need to cover up.

And truth extends to the exaggeration, the innuendo and the implication. If you refrain from twisting the truth, you never need to unravel a relationship gone awry.

Impossibilities vanish
when a man and his
God confront
a mountain.

. . . but with God all things are possible.
Matthew 19:26 (KJV)

Walking on the moon was once considered to be impossible, and yet Neil Armstrong and Buzz Aldrin did just that on July 20, 1969. Michael Collins, the astronaut who remained aloft in *Columbia*, writes of another seeming impossibility overcome that day:

'They hadn't been out on the surface very long when the three of us got a big surprise. The President of the United States began talking on the radio! Mr Nixon said, "Neil and Buzz, I am talking to you by telephone from the Oval Office at the White House, and this certainly has to be the most historic telephone call ever made . . . Because of what you have done, the heavens have become a part of man's world. As you talk to us from the Sea of Tranquility, it inspires us to redouble our efforts to bring peace and tranquillity to Earth." '

Our prayers are like an unseen communication link that spans heaven and earth. Things once regarded as impossible become possible when that link is firmly established.

For many little girls,
life with father is
dress rehearsal for
love and marriage.

*Whatever you have learned or received
or heard from me, or seen in me –
put it into practice. And the
God of peace will be with you.*
Philippians 4:9 (NIV)

In one of his short stories, O. Henry tells of an only child whose mother had died. Her father would come home from work, fix their meal and then sit down with his paper and pipe, put his feet up on the hassock, and read. When the little girl, starved for companionship after being home alone all day would ask, 'Father, would you play with me?' he would reply, 'No, I'm too tired,' or, 'No, I'm too busy.' He usually advised her, 'Go out on the street and play.'

This little girl heard her father's advice to go out on the street and play so often that she literally grew up on the streets outside her home. She eventually became a streetwalker, a prostitute – to her dying day she continued to search on the streets for affection and someone with whom to keep company.

Neglect is one of the most devastating ways a parent can abuse a child. Tell your child that you love her, and spend time with her so she won't have to find someone else who will.

My primary role is
not to be the boss and
just look good, but to be
a servant leader who
enables and enhances my
family to be their best.

*Let this mind be in you, which was also
in Christ Jesus . . . [who] took upon
him the form of a servant . . .*
Philippians 2:5,7 (KJV)

During the Civil War, the son of a Quaker family in Pennsylvania left home against his father's wishes and enlisted in the cause of the North. Time passed and no word was heard from him. One night the father had a dream that his son was in great need. The next morning the father left the farm and after discovering where the troops had been sent, made his way by horse-drawn buggy to the battlefield. In asking about his son, he learned that the troops had been under heavy fire earlier in the day and many had fallen wounded. The father asked for permission to try to find his son, and the commander wearily granted it.

The father searched late into the afternoon and when it was dark, he lit a lantern and went from person to person, letting the light fall across the faces of the wounded young men. As he stumbled among the bodies, he began calling loudly after every few steps, 'Jonathan Smythe, thy father seeketh after thee.' Diligently he kept at his search until finally he heard a very faint, barely audible reply, 'Father, over here.' And then he added, 'I knew you would come.'

Can your child count on you to find him and come to his aid when he is in distress? A true servant always looks for a way to help and give comfort.

We too often love things
and use people,
when we should be using
things and loving people.

*Be devoted to one another in
brotherly love. Honour one another
above yourselves.*
Romans 12:10 (NIV)

When Andrew Carnegie sold his steel company in 1901, his share of the sale price ensured that he would receive $1 million a month, for life. What did he do with the money? He gave it away!

During the last eighteen years of his life, Carnegie gave away nearly $350 million. He believed that the lives of rich men are divided into two parts: the first for getting money, the second for giving it away. He also believed that rich men could make a better world, and he focused his giving very specifically. He helped pay for 2,800 libraries in the United States and the British Empire, at a cost of $60 million. Carnegie believed that children like himself could improve their minds by reading, even if they could not stay in school very long. He gave $30 million to American and British universities, mostly to smaller schools, because he wanted the children of poor workers to have a chance for a college education. He also gave large amounts of money for pensions for teachers and steelworkers. And, he made possible the Carnegie Hero Fund, which gave awards for bravery in time of peace.

Carnegie truly was a man who used what he had earned to show love to others.

The kind of man who thinks that helping with the dishes is beneath him will also think that helping with the baby is beneath him, and then he certainly is not going to be a very successful father.

. . . but whoever wishes to become great among you shall be your servant.
Matthew 20:26 (NAS)

The great Protestant reformer Martin Luther once wrote this about the role of a husband and father: 'Along comes the clever harlot, namely natural reason, looks at married life, turns up her nose and says: "Why must I rock the baby, wash its nappies, change its bed, smell its odour, heal its rash, take care of this and take care of that, do this and do that? It is better to remain single and live a quiet and carefree life. I will become a priest or a nun and tell my children to do the same."

'But what does the Christian faith say? The father opens his eyes, looks at these lowly, distasteful and despised things and knows that they are adorned with divine approval as with the most precious gold and silver. God, with His angels and creatures, will smile – not because nappies are washed, but because it is done in faith.'

Even the most mundane task can become an act of 'worship' – an act of service rendered not to others, but as unto God. As you help your wife and children with the simplest of chores, imagine that you are doing the task for the benefit of the Lord Jesus Himself.

The best things you
can give children,
next to good habits,
are good memories.

The memory of the righteous is blessed . . .
Proverbs 10:7 (NAS)

Two boys were dressed and ready to go. In fact, they had been ready for more than an hour. Excitement flooded their faces and all their talk was about only one thing: their father had promised to take them to the circus that afternoon!

As planned, Dad came home from work after lunch and quickly changed into casual clothing. Then, just as the three of them were about to leave the house, the phone rang. The boys listened as their father talked with the person on the other end of the line. Bit by bit, their faces began to fall. This was obviously a business call, and some urgent matter was requiring their father's attention in town. Disappointment rolled into the room like a dark cloud. Their mother also overheard what she thought was the inevitable change of plans. And then, to the surprise of all, they heard Dad say, 'No, I won't be down. It will just have to wait until morning.'

Hanging up the phone he called for the boys to meet him at the car as he turned to kiss his wife good-bye. She smiled and with a twinge of fear that he may have made the wrong decision, she said, 'The circus keeps coming back, you know.' The father replied, 'Yes, I know. But childhood doesn't.'

Honour is better than honours.

*. . . for them that honour me
I will honour . . .*
1 Samuel 2:30 (KJV)

Francis I, King of France from 1515–1547, spent some twenty-seven years of his reign at war with Charles V, the German Emperor and the King of Spain. The hostility began in 1521 and two years later, while Francis was pursuing his enemies, he received word that his wife had died. Shortly thereafter, he received notice that his second daughter had also died.

During the battle of Pavia in 1525, Francis was defeated, wounded and taken prisoner. In a letter to his mother from prison, he wrote, 'Madame, to inform you of the rest of my misfortune, I have nothing left to me save my honour and my life.'

The Emperor demanded one-third of France, renunciation of France's claim to Italy and the return of Charles de Bourbon's provinces, along with Provence. Francis did the honourable thing and refused, saying, 'I am resolved to endure prison for as long as God wills rather than accept terms injurious to my kingdom.' Francis retained honour to the end, not only for himself, but for all Frenchmen.

There may be times in our lives when all we have left is our honour and our lives. Even so, that is sufficient, for honour transcends life itself. It passes into history even as we pass into eternity.

It may be hard on some fathers not to have a son, but it is much harder on a boy not to have a father.

*Whenever you possibly can,
do good to those who need it.*
Proverbs 3:27 (GNB)

A very successful Christian businessman had one son. He was very proud of this boy who seemed to have grown to be a well-educated and well-respected gentleman. Then one day the son was arrested for embezzlement and upon trial was found guilty. All through the trial and up to the rendering of the verdict, the young man appeared unconcerned and nonchalant. He seemed more proud than humbled or broken by the experience.

Then the verdict was brought in. The judge told the young man to stand for the sentence, which he did – still somewhat cocky in demeanour. He glanced around the courtroom and to his amazement he saw that his father was also standing. His father had realized that he, too, was involved – not with what the boy had done, but with what the boy had become.

The young man saw his father – an honest man with a clear conscience – bowed low with sorrow and shame to receive, as though it were for himself, his son's sentence. The son wept bitterly and for the first time, truly repented of his crime.

The future of a boy cannot be separated from the present – or the presence – of his father.

It is not what a man
does that determines
whether his work is
sacred or secular, it is
why he does it.

Whatever you do, work at it
with all your heart, as working
for the Lord, not for men . . .
It is the Lord Christ you are serving.
Colossians 3:23,24 (NIV)

Legend has it that a missionary was swept overboard while travelling on very high and rough seas, and was subsequently washed up on a beach at the edge of a remote native village. Nearly dead from exposure and lack of food and fresh water, he was found by the people of the village and nursed back to health. He lived among them for twenty years, quietly adapting to their culture and working alongside them. He preached no sermons and made no personal faith claim. He neither read nor recited Scripture to them.

But . . . when people were sick, he sat with them, sometimes all night. When people were hungry, he fed them. When people were lonely, he gave a listening ear. He taught the ignorant and always took the side of the one who had been wronged.

The day came when missionaries entered this village and began talking to the people about a man named Jesus. After listening for a while to their story, the native people began insisting that Jesus had already been living in their village for many years. 'Come,' one of them said, 'we'll introduce you to Him.' The missionaries were led to a hut where they found their long-lost companion!

Why we work always determines *how* we live.

The most effective
thing we can do
for our children and
families is pray for them.

*Devote yourselves to prayer, keeping alert
in it with an attitude of thanksgiving.*
Colossians 4:2 (NAS)

Spiritual giants in every age have agreed about prayer: more is better. The founder of Methodism, John Wesley, spent one to two hours a day in private communication with God. Both Martin Luther and Bishop Francis Asbury believed two hours of prayer a day was a minimum. The great Scottish preacher, John Welch, regularly prayed eight to ten hours a day – and then often awoke in the middle of the night to continue his conversation with the Lord.

None of these men were ivory-tower contemplatives with nothing else to do. Asbury for example, travelled some 300,000 miles, mostly on horseback, to build the American Methodist Church. All advocated that a person combine prayer with work, including praying as one works.

Today, many parents lead such busy lives they often think they have no time for prayer on behalf of their families. Yet, the most potent thing a parent can do is to pray. As you drive to work, walk from place to place, do mundane chores . . . talk to God at length about each child. Thank God for your children. Listen for His advice. The change in your child and your relationship with your child is likely to be remarkable, even miraculous!

A father should never make distinctions between his children.

For God does not show favouritism.

Romans 2:11 (NIV)

A Sunday school superintendent was registering two new boys in Sunday school. She asked their ages and birthdays so she could place them in the appropriate classes. The bolder of the two replied, 'We're both seven. My birthday is April 8 and my brother's birthday is April 20.' The superintendent replied, 'But that's not possible, boys.' The quieter brother spoke up. 'No, it's true. One of us is adopted.'

'Oh?' asked the superintendent, not convinced. 'Which one?' The two brothers looked at each other and smiled. The bolder one said, 'We asked Dad that same question a while ago, but he just looked at us and said he loved us both equally and he couldn't remember any more which one of us was adopted.'

What a wonderful analogy of God's love! The Apostle Paul wrote to the Romans: 'Now if we are [God's] children, then we are heirs – heirs of God and co-heirs with Christ . . .' (Romans 8:17, NIV). In essence, as adopted sons and daughters of God, we fully share in the inheritance of His begotten Son, Jesus. If our Heavenly Father can love us on equal footing with His beloved Son, surely we can love our children equally and show no partiality in the blessings – or privileges – we extend to them.

Character is what you are in the dark.

*The integrity of the upright
shall guide them . . .*
Proverbs 11:3 (KJV)

A nurse named Carol was once the victim of an elaborate hoax. A con artist came to her claiming to know a famous rock star. He asked the nurse to loan him her car so he could bring the rock star from a nearby auditorium to visit the quadriplegic children and adults under her care. He was so convincing and gave so many details that Carol allowed him to take her car. Not only did Carol lose her car, but she lost the respect of many of her patients whom she had told about the impending visit.

When the rock star heard how his name had been misused, he decided to take action. Without media attention, he made a surprise visit to the hospital. He met Carol and, with her by his side, he spoke warmly to her patients, signing autographs, passing out copies of his latest recording and giving away posters as he greeted each one personally. Nurse Carol said after his visit, 'You should have seen the smiles on their faces. He's more than a rock star to them now. He's become their friend.'

The 'onstage' character played by many people is not the same as the person's backstage persona. It's backstage character that truly counts, however. And in the end, it's the only character worth playing!

One hundred years
from now it won't matter
if you got that big break . . .
or finally got a Mercedes.
It will greatly matter, one
hundred years from now,
that you made a commitment
to Jesus Christ.

What profit is there if you gain the whole
world – and lose eternal life?
Matthew 16:26 (TLB)

In *A Christmas Carol*, Charles Dickens' character Scrooge rails to his nephew about Christmas: 'What's Christmas time . . . but a time for paying bills without money; a time for finding yourself a year older, and not an hour richer; a time for balancing your books? . . . If I could work my will, every idiot who goes about with "Merry Christmas," on his lips, should be boiled with his own pudding, and buried with a stake of holly through his heart. He should!' Scrooge then gives his opinion about his nephew's celebration of Christmas, 'Much good it has ever done you!'

At this, Scrooge's nephew replies, 'There are many things from which I might have derived good, by which I have not profited, I dare say Christmas among the rest. But I am sure I have always thought of Christmas time . . . as a good time: a kind, forgiving, charitable, pleasant time: the only time I know of, in the long calendar of the year, when men and women seem by one consent to open their shut-up hearts freely . . . And therefore, uncle, though it has never put a scrap of gold or silver in my pocket, I believe that it *has* done me good, and *will* do me good.'

The *unseen* reward of making a commitment to Christ *now* does not make it less valuable in eternity!

You cannot teach a child to
take care of himself unless
you will let him try . . .
He will make
mistakes and out
of these mistakes
will come his wisdom.

All your sons will be taught by the LORD,
and great will be your children's peace.
Isaiah 54:13 (NIV)

Two hunters chartered a plane to fly them into a remote region in Canada so that they might hunt for elk. The plane returned for them a few days later. Indeed, the hunt had been successful – the two hunters had six elk to show for their effort.

When the pilot explained to them that his plane could only carry four of the elk, the hunters protested, 'But the plane that we chartered last year was exactly like this one. It had the same horsepower, the weather was similar and we took out six elk then.'

Hearing this, the pilot reluctantly agreed to load all six elk. The plane struggled during take off, but was unable to gain sufficient altitude to climb out of the valley. It crashed near the top of a mountain. To their great fortune, all three men survived.

As the hunters stumbled out of the wreckage, one of them asked the dazed pilot, 'Do you know where we are?' He mumbled, 'No.' The other hunter, however, looked around and said confidently, 'I think we're about a mile from where we crashed last year!'

Mistakes are meant to lead to wisdom, not to future error. Teach your child to learn lessons from his skinned knees and bruised elbows. He'll have less pain and fewer scrapes in his adult life.

He who sacrifices
his conscience to
ambition burns a picture
to obtain the ashes.

Keep your faith and a clear conscience.
Some men have not listened to their
conscience and have made a
ruin of their faith.
1 Timothy 1:19 (GNB)

Bubba Smith became famous not only for his performance on the football field, but perhaps even more so, for his performances on television as a spokesman for a brewery. The day came, however, when Bubba swore off booze.

Now, Bubba never did drink. Still, he went on selling countless kegs of beer by making clever beer commercials. He may be the first athlete ever to give up a highly lucrative, easy and amusing job because he felt it was morally wrong. Why did he take this step?

Bubba was invited to be the grand marshall of a major university's homecoming parade, and as he rode around the field during halftime, he heard drunken college fans yelling, 'Tastes great!' while others shouted, 'Less filling.' In Bubba's opinion, they *should* have been yelling, 'Go, State!' or, 'Get 'em, Bubba.'

Bubba Smith realized in a matter of moments that he was encouraging others to do something that he himself chose not to do. When young school children began approaching him on the streets reciting his commercials verbatim, Bubba hung up his commercial career, saying simply, 'I had to stop compromising my principles.' May a clear conscience always be more valuable to us than man-made rewards!

The ultimate measure of a
man is not where he stands
in moments of comfort
and convenience,
but where he stands at
times of challenge
and controversy.

*If you falter in times of trouble,
how small is your strength!*
Proverbs 24:10 (NIV)

68

In 1955, the black people of Montgomery, Alabama, were angry when Rosa Parks was arrested for sitting in the front of a bus – the area supposedly reserved for white passengers only. The 27-year-old minister of the Dexter Avenue Baptist Church in Montgomery met with other ministers to decide on a course of action. They urged their fellow blacks not to ride the city's buses on December 5. The bus boycott, however, lasted 382 days. The ministers repeatedly urged blacks to remain peaceful and calm.

The publicity surrounding the bus boycott made the young minister, Martin Luther King, Jr., famous internationally almost overnight. Then he became not only a spokesman, but a target. A bomb exploded on his front porch. Nobody was hurt, but a crowd of more than a thousand blacks gathered in anger. King spoke from the smoking ruins of his porch, saying, 'Be peaceful. I want you to love your enemies.'

It's one thing to advocate change when you are speaking behind a microphone. It's another to stand for change when your wife and children barely escape death. But King was a man of deep convictions, and in his standing in crisis, an even stronger message was sent to those who opposed civil rights for blacks.

If you tell the truth, you don't have to remember anything.

A truthful witness gives honest testimony, but a false witness tells lies.

Proverbs 12:17 (NIV)

Four senior school boys skipped their first period class one morning in order to joyride around town. Coming in late, they all apologized profusely to the teacher, claiming that they had had a flat tyre on the way to school. They gave a long litany of complications they had experienced in repairing it.

The teacher smiled sympathetically and then explained that they had missed a quiz given during the first period. 'Can't we make it up?' one of the boys asked. Another chimed in, 'It wasn't our fault.' A third added, 'Surely you can't hold a flat tyre against us.'

The teacher said, 'Well, all right.' She then told the boys to take empty seats in the four corners of the room, to take out paper and pencil, and answer this one question:

'Which tyre was flat?'

There's no substitute for telling the truth!

Sometimes we think that if we only tell a little 'white lie' we really aren't hurting anybody. In fact, we are – ourselves – for in telling lies of any size we are developing a pattern in our lives of mixing black with white. Eventually we will see only grey and be unable to discern clearly the truth of what is right and wrong.

When we love
something it is of
value to us, and when
something is of value
to us we spend
time with it, time
enjoying it and time
taking care of it.

*And I will very gladly spend
and be spent for you . . .*
2 Corinthians 12:15 (KJV)

Imagine for a moment that your bank suddenly announced this as its new policy: Every morning your account is going to be credited with £86,400. You can carry no balance from day to day. Every evening, your account will be cancelled and whatever amount of your account you have failed to use during the day will be returned to the bank.

What would you do? Why you'd draw out every penny of the £86,400 each day and spend it, save it or invest it as wisely as possible. Before long, you could be a very wealthy person, indeed!

Actually you have a bank account with a similar policy. It is called 'Time'. Every morning, you are given the prospect of 86,400 seconds. At the close of that twenty-four hour period, the moments you have failed to withdraw and invest to good purpose are ruled off your ledger. Time carries no balances from day to day. It allows no overdrafts. Each day a new account is opened for you. If you fail to withdraw and use the day's deposit, the loss is yours.

Those who truly love life use time to the maximum. They make their days count rather than counting their days!

Nothing I've ever
done has given
me more joys and
rewards than being a
father to my children.

Children are a gift from God;
they are his reward.
Psalm 127:3 (TLB)

When television journalist Bob Greene was first asked by others how it felt to be a new father, he recalls, 'Normally, I shrug the question off; it's so complicated and so consuming that I don't feel I can do it justice with a glib reply I usually just say "Yeah, it's great," and let it go at that.'

One day however, he truly expressed to two friends how he *felt*. He writes in his book, *Good Morning, Merry Sunshine:* 'I don't even know how to explain it. I've been spending time on the road ever since I started working for a living. I've complained about it a lot, but I've really liked the idea of it. Going into different cities, sleeping in hotels, meeting strange people . . . I've really liked it.

'Now, though, when I'm gone . . . I physically *ache* for missing my daughter. It never seems that any story is important enough to make me not see her for another day. I know I still go out on the road all the time – I wonder if I'm fooling myself – but missing her is not some vague concept in my mind. It actually hurts when I think that she's at home and I'm not with her. Sometimes I fall asleep thinking about it.'

Sometimes the feelings of being a dad are beyond words. And that's OK

Trust in yourself and you are doomed to disappointment . . . trust in money and you may have it taken from you . . . but trust in God, and you are never to be confounded in time or eternity.

It is better to take refuge in the LORD than to trust in man.

Psalm 118:8 (NIV)

Eight of the most powerful money magnates in the world gathered for a meeting at the Edgewater Beach Hotel in Chicago, Illinois, in 1923. The combined resources and assets of these eight men tallied more than the US Treasury that year. In the group were Charles Schwab, president of a steel company, Richard Whitney, president of the New York Stock Exchange and Arthur Cutton, a wheat speculator. Albert Fall was a presidential cabinet member, a personally wealthy man. Jesse Livermore was the greatest Wall Street 'bear' in his generation. Leon Fraser was the president of the International Bank of Settlements and Ivan Krueger headed the largest monopoly in the nation. An impressive gathering of financial eagles!

What happened to these men in later years? Schwab died penniless. Whitney served a life sentence in Sing Sing Prison. Cutton became insolvent. Fall was pardoned from a federal prison so he might die at home. Fraser, Livermore and Krueger committed suicide. Seven of these eight extremely rich men had lives that turned out disastrous.

What a mistake it is to think that you control what you have – be it life or money.

The superior man . . .
stands erect by
bending above
the fallen. He rises
by lifting others.

*We urge you, brethren, admonish the
unruly, encourage the fainthearted, help
the weak, be patient with everyone.*
1 Thessalonians 5:14 (NAS)

Andrew Davison had a rare and life-impacting opportunity to visit Dr Albert Schweitzer at his jungle hospital on the banks of the Ogowe River. For three days, he engaged in leisurely conversation with the great humanitarian, theologian, musician and physician. He reported later that his three-day visit had a deep and profound effect on him. In writing of his visit, however, Davison didn't relay the content of their conversations, but rather, this incident:

'It was about eleven in the morning. The equatorial sun was beating down mercilessly and we were walking up a hill with Dr Schweitzer. Suddenly he left us and strode across the slope of the hill to a place where an African woman was struggling upward with a huge armload of wood for the cookfires. I watched with both admiration and concern as the eighty-five-year-old man took the entire load of wood and carried it on up the hill for the relieved woman. When we all reached the top of the hill, one of the members of our group asked Dr Schweitzer why he did things like that, implying that in that heat and at his age he should not. Albert Schweitzer, looking right at all of us and pointing to the woman, said simply "No one should ever have to carry a burden like that alone." '

Children spell
'love' . . . T~I~M~E.

Don't be fools; be wise:
make the most of every opportunity
you have for doing good.
Ephesians 5:16 (TLB)

Every time baseball player Tim Burke left to go on the road, he found it more difficult to leave his wife and their three children. Stephanie, age 4, confessed to her father why she was upset one day, 'You go away all the time to play baseball.' Though he did his best to console her, he felt as if he was consoling himself.

When spring training rolled around the next year, Tim's heart wasn't in it. He asked his wife, 'How would you feel about my retiring?' Although his wife was scared he might regret the decision, especially since baseball was Tim's first and only job, she also was scared at the toll another season might have on their family. By the second week of spring training, however, Tim had reached a decision. He announced to his manager, 'I've decided to retire today.'

After he had cleared out his locker, reporters gathered around to ask, 'Why?' Tim gave this eloquent answer: 'My family needs me more than the Reds do. Baseball's going to do just fine without me, but I'm the only father my children have. I'm the only husband my wife has. And they need me now.'

Many men dream of living the life of a professional ball player. Tim Burke gave it up for the life *he* dreamed about.

It is better to bind
your children to you
by a feeling of respect,
and by gentleness,
than by fear.

Your gentleness has made me great.
Psalm 18:35 (NKJ)

A mother and her children went looking for a Father's Day card one year. Suddenly the youngest of the four children shouted with glee, 'I found it! I found it!' After each of the children had read the card, they passed it to Mum with a unanimous vote – and fortunately a laugh: 'This is it, Mum! This is for Dad.'

The woman took the card and saw that it had been written to resemble a small child's block printing. On the front of the card was a little boy with dirty trainers. They were untied, naturally. His cap was twisted to one side, his jeans were torn. He looked dirty and sweaty from playing hard outside. He was holding on to the handle of a little wagon, loaded with broken toys and a cricket bat. In his hip pocket was a catapult. He had a black eye and a plaster stuck on his arm. The front of the card read:

'Dad, I'll never forget that little prayer you said for me every day.' And then on the inside of the card were these words: 'God help you if you ever do that again!'

Discipline your child as a display of power and they'll fear you – and eventually distrust you – and then hate you. Discipline your child out of love and with love, however, and they'll respect you for it.

The best time for
you to hold your tongue
is the time you feel
you must say
something or bust.

*Don't talk so much. You keep putting
your foot in your mouth.
Be sensible and turn off the flow!*
Proverbs 10:19 (TLB)

Many analogies have been given for the 'untamed tongue'. Quarles likened it to a drawn sword that takes a person prisoner: 'A word unspoken is like the sword in the scabbard, thine; if vented, thy sword is in another's hand.'

Others have described evil-speaking as:

• *a freezing wind* – one that seals up the sparkling waters and kills the tender flowers and shoots of growth. In similar fashion, bitter and hate-filled words bind up the hearts of men and cause love to cease to flourish.

• *a fox with a firebrand tied to its tail*, sent out among the standing corn just as in the days of Samson and the Philistines. So gossip spreads without control or reason.

• *a pistol fired in the mountains*, the echo of which is intensified until it sounds like thunder.

• *a snowball that gathers size* as it rolls down a mountain.

Perhaps the greatest analogy, however, is one given by a little child who came running to her parent in tears. 'Did your friend hurt you?' the parent asked.

'Yes,' said the girl. 'Where?' the parent asked again. 'Right here,' said the child, pointing to her heart.

Laughter is the shortest distance between two people.

The light in the eyes (of him whose heart is joyful) rejoices the hearts of others.
Proverbs 15:30 (AMP)

One day Dr Bernie S. Siegel, author of *Peace, Love and Healing*, got a call from a policeman friend, who began talking about all of the horrors in the world and about the despair of his own life. He finally said morbidly, 'I have nothing to live for. I just called to say goodbye.'

'Goodbye?' asked Siegel. 'What do you mean?'

The friend said in a flat voice, 'I'm going to commit suicide. I just called to say goodbye.'

Without a pause, Siegel quipped, 'Well, if you do, I'll never speak to you again.'

Astounded – and jolted from his deep malaise – the policeman started to chuckle. Instead of shooting himself as he had planned, he decided to go see his friend Bernie for a heart-to-heart chat.

It's very, very difficult to remain angry at someone who makes you laugh. It's hard to remain sad around a person who makes you giggle. It's extremely difficult to hold a grudge against a person who brings a smile to your face. It's almost impossible to stay frightened if you're with a person who causes you to chuckle.

Laughter is a tie that binds hearts together.

If you keep telling
your son something's
wrong with him,
sooner or later he'll
believe it. Follow
every, 'That's wrong'
by saying what's right.

*My brothers and sisters: I myself feel
sure that you are full of goodness,
that you have all knowledge, and
that you are able to teach one another.*
Romans 15:14 (GNB)

While a man was holidaying in the Bahamas, he was sightseeing one afternoon when he noticed a crowd gathered at the end of a pier. He went closer to investigate the commotion and discovered that a young man was making last-minute preparations for a solo journey around the world in a homemade boat. Without exception, everyone on the pier was trying to talk him out of his voyage, telling him everything they thought could go wrong with the trip: 'The sun will grill you!' 'You don't have enough food.' 'That boat won't make it through a storm.' 'You'll never make it.'

In spite of all these dire warnings, the optimistic and ambitious young sailor pushed away from the dock. As he sailed away, the observer ran to the end of the pier and with both arms waving wildly he shouted: 'BON VOYAGE! You're really something! We're with you. We're proud of you!'

After the boat was out of earshot, he turned and found the crowd staring at him in disbelief. 'Do you really believe that?' one man asked. The tourist replied, 'I don't know. But if he gets into trouble, I hope he remembers my words, not yours.'

Say to your child, 'Go for it!' And then pray they make it.

You can't do much
about your ancestors
but you can influence
your descendants
enormously.

*. . . but as for me and my house,
we will serve the LORD.*
Joshua 24:15 (KJV)

Consider the lives of two men. One of them, Max Jukes, lived in New York. He did not believe in Christ or give Christian training to his children. He refused to take his children to church even when they asked to attend. He had 1,026 descendants – 300 of whom were sent to prison for an average term of thirteen years. Some 190 were public prostitutes and 680 were admitted alcoholics. His family members have cost the state in excess of $420,000 – thus far – and they have made no known positive contributions to society.

Jonathan Edwards lived in the same state and at the same time. He loved the Lord and saw that his children were in church every Sunday. He served the Lord to the best of his ability. Of his 929 descendants, 430 were ministers, 86 became university professors, 13 became university presidents, 75 wrote positive books, 7 were elected to the US Congress, and one served as vice-president of the United States. His family never cost the state one cent but contributed immeasurably to the common good.

Ask yourself: if my family tree began with me, what fruit might it bear two hundred years from now?

Every dad is the
family role model,
whether he wants
the job or not.

*. . . in order to offer ourselves as
a model for you, so that you would
follow our example.*
2 Thessalonians 3:9 (NAS)

Famous baseball pitcher, Orel Hershiser, is often regarded as a role model for young people in America today. But who was his primary role model? In his book *Out of the Blue*, Hershiser describes his role model as a man who was very competitive, yet generous and a gentleman. 'In everything he does,' says Hershiser, 'he wants to win . . . Sometimes he would compete only with himself. I saw that side of him even in how he cleaned the garage. He took care of every detail and put everything in its place.'

He always commended and rewarded those who did a good job. A perfectionist, he often demanded that a job be done repeatedly but even so, he gave a pat on the back in encouragement. He didn't mind pain and he didn't mind work. And he had a grand habit of asking 'why?' When others might say in the face of a weather prediction of rain, 'There goes our golf date tomorrow,' he would say instead, 'Why? Does the weatherman have to be right? We don't know what tomorrow will be like. The storm may pass through. Let's plan on playing and see if it works out.' He was a stubborn optimistic, with a never-give-up attitude.

Who was this superlative role model? His dad!

Children are like clocks; they must be allowed to run.

*Fathers . . . do not be hard on them
(children) or harass them;
lest they become discouraged . . .*
Colossians 3:21 (AMP)

For a number of years, 'flea circuses' were quite popular. Today few people have seen one, much less know how fleas come to be trained.

When fleas are first put into a jar, they jump wildly. Since they are incredible jumpers, a lid must be put on even a large jar in order to keep them contained. Still, they continue to jump, hitting their heads on the lid again and again. Over time, however, the fleas no longer jump as high they did initially. Most of them jump to a height that is just a fraction of an inch from beneath the lid.

At this point, a flea trainer can remove the lid from the jar. The fleas will continue to jump, but now, they no longer jump out of the jar. The reason is simple. They have conditioned themselves to jump only so high. Once conditioned to jump to that height, that's all they can do!

They will never again regain their ability to jump higher.

Have you 'capped' your child in some way today? Have you built a ceiling so low for your child that he is forever hitting his head? Remove that lid quickly! Otherwise, you may forever stunt his concept of his own potential!

The child that never
learned to obey his
parents in the home
will not obey God or
man out of the home.

*Children, obey your parents
in the Lord: for this is right.*
Ephesians 6:1 (KJV)

Susannah Wesley, mother of John and Charles Wesley, was a God-fearing mother of seventeen children. Many of her principles for child training appear in John Wesley's journal, such as:

'When turned a year old (and some before), they were taught to fear the rod and to cry softly; by which means they escaped abundance of correction they might otherwise have had; and that most odious noise of the crying of children was rarely heard in the house; but the family usually lived in as much quietness as if there had not been a child among them.

'In order to form the minds of children, the first thing to be done is to conquer the will, and bring them to an obedient temper. To inform the understanding is a work of time, and must with children proceed by slow degrees as they are able to bear it; but subjecting the will is a thing which must be done at once; and the sooner the better. For by neglecting timely correction they will contract a stubbornness and obstinacy which is hardly ever after conquered.

'Self-will is the root of all sin and misery, so whatever cherishes this in children insures their after-wretchedness; whatever checks and mortifies it promotes their future happiness.'

By profession I am a
soldier and take pride in
that fact, but I am
prouder to be a father.

I have great confidence in you;
I take great pride in you . . .
2 Corinthians 7:4 (NIV)

Navy fighter pilot, Lt Cmdr John E. Bartocci, was stationed aboard the aircraft carrier *Bon Homme Richard* during the Vietnam War. His letters home during 1976 reveal his great love for his family:

31 Jan. Three years of shore duty were wonderful. The children's characters have really taken shape. I know them so much better now, and that makes leaving so much more difficult.

6 May. After the pressures of this air war, I know what a treasure the serenity of the family is. I long to feel the children's arms around me, to play the role of the lion with his cubs. Tears come to my eyes when I think how I want to be with my children, playing with them, explaining things to them, trying to give them some of myself.

12 June. I'm looking at the beautiful pictures you sent me of the children. I see such hope in their eyes. I want so much to hold them in my arms . . . to be there to influence my children, to bring out their good qualities. What greater success can a father ask?

Six weeks later, Bartocci was killed when his aircraft crashed while returning from a night mission.

Hug your children today. Tell them how much you love them. Learn to treasure and make the most out of every day you have with your children.

The strongest evidence of love is sacrifice.

For God so loved the world that He gave His only begotten Son, that whoever believes in Him should not perish but have everlasting life.
John 3:16 (NKJ)

Andrew Wyermann's favourite Christmas memory took place when he was seven years old. He recalls, 'Early on Christmas Eve, my mother took my brother and me out for a treat. It was her way to get us out of our fifth-floor apartment in the Bronx while my father prepared for the evening festivity. As we climbed the stairs back to the apartment, the shrill sound of a whistle filled the hallway. What was that, and where did it come from? Our pace quickened and a second burst of the whistle could be heard. We dashed into the apartment. There was my father playing engineer with the biggest Lionel train ever made. It was so magnificent, so unexpected, so wonderful!

'Some fifty years later, I still have the train set and cherish it . . . The train is a warm reminder of the greater gift my parents gave me. This gift has nothing to do with any material advantages, or even with any piece of sage advice. Unconditional love was their gift. I never doubted their care for me, and from such grace sprang my own capacity to truth. It was years later that I fully understood the gift my parents gave me had its source in God's gift of the Child to us all. The sound of the whistle and the song of the angels have become one and the same.'

Govern a family as you would cook a small fish – very gently.

And a servant of the Lord must not quarrel but be gentle to all . . .
2 Timothy 2:24 (NKJ)

Adelaida Blanton tells of a 'five minute rule' that she had in her home when she was a child. 'What it meant,' she explains, 'was that we were all to be ready for school five minutes before we actually had to leave.

'We were a large family and that extra five minutes was prayer time for Mother and us children. The place was wherever Mother happened to be when we were all ready to leave. Sometimes it was the kitchen, other times the living room or bedroom, or even out on the porch. But we all kneeled while Mother asked a blessing on each of us individually and thanked the Lord for His provision for us. Often all of our names were spoken and some special blessing asked for each.

'If a neighbourhood child dropped in to walk to school with us (and neighbours often did), they were included in our prayer circle, too.

'When the prayer was finished, there came a kiss for each, and we were off.

'Those were Five Important Minutes to each of us.'

Aren't there five minutes you can find today for a gentle and godly time out with your child?

Words have an
awesome impact. The
impressions made by a
father's voice can set in
motion an entire
trend of life.

*What you say can preserve life
or destroy it; so you must accept
the consequences of your words.*
Proverbs 18:21 (GNB)

Arthur's father only had to give an order once and one of his commandments was, 'There's to be no hanging around. If he ain't workin' or someplace special, a man is supposed to be home.' Arthur and his brother Johnnie were taught to work hard and love the family. Arthur's dad also said, 'You gain by helping others.' To match deed to word, he would take his sons with him to deliver old clothes, food and wood to families in need. He also said, 'You don't get nowhere by making enemies.' Arthur never forgot.

As an internationally renowned tennis player, Arthur Ashe arose at five o'clock on summer days, hit 500 balls, ate breakfast and then hit 500 more. He was known for his drive on the court and his gentleman's demeanour off the court. He built a strong family. His wife, Jeanne, and his daughter, Camera, were the light of his life. He started the Safe Passage Foundation to help poor youngsters learn tennis, golf and fencing, and also improve their scholastic skills. And all his adult life, he fought to bring blacks and whites closer together.

What Arthur Ashe, Sr., said, he did. And so, too, Arthur Ashe, Jr.

Like father, like son:
Every good tree
maketh good fruits.

So, every sound tree bears good fruit . . .
Matthew 7:17 (RSV)

A little boy was given a globe of the world as a gift. He especially liked the fact that it had a light in it. The little boy put it in a secure spot in his room and not only looked at it often during the day, but used it as a night light in his room at bedtime.

One night his parents were debating a point of geography when one of them remembered the globe in their son's room. Dad went to get the globe for reference, quietly tiptoeing into his child's semi-dark room and unplugging it. Just as he was almost out the door, his son called to him in a sleepy voice, 'Daddy what are you doing with my world?'

What an important question for any father to ask himself! What is it that you are doing with your child's world today? How are you managing it? What are you planting in it? How are you developing it? . . . But equally importantly, how are you dealing with your own world? Your child isn't likely to reflect any greater spiritual, moral or ethical values than those you hold. He isn't likely to learn what you don't teach or encourage. He isn't likely to be much different than you! Because, to a great extent . . . you *are* his world. What you do with your own life is the foundation on which his world is built.

An infallible way to
make your child
miserable is to satisfy
all his demands.

The rod of correction imparts wisdom,
but a child left to himself
disgraces his mother.
Proverbs 29:15 (NIV)

The sheriff's office in a Texas city once published and distributed a list of rules entitled 'How to Raise a Juvenile Delinquent in Your Own Family'. Among the advice given were these admonitions:

Begin with infancy to give the child everything he wants.

This will insure his believing that the world owes him a living.

Pick up everything he leaves lying around.

This will teach him he can always throw off responsibility on others.

Take his part against neighbours, teachers and policemen. Teach him that they are all prejudiced against your child and that he is a 'free spirit' and never wrong.

This will instil in him that he is to have no regard for any person who ever attempts to correct him or limit his behaviour.

Finally prepare youself for a life of grief. You're going to have it.

A child who never hears the word *no* has a limited understanding of the word *yes*.

Performance under
stress is one test of
effective leadership.
It may also be the
proof of accomplishment
when it comes to evaluating
the quality of a father.

*Cast your burden on the LORD, and he
will sustain you; he will never permit
the righteous to be moved.*
Psalm 55:22 (RSV)

Few doubt the bravery and military skill of General Robert E. Lee. As commander of the army of Northern Virginia, he was known for shrewdness, fast thinking, an instinct for the counterpunch. He had a keen ability to learn from mistakes and to improvise under the pressure of necessity. Military students still study the way in which he took command and set a course with such mastery that every battle he fought became part of a single campaign.

What many don't know, however, is that Lee had no real taste for war. He much preferred to be at home, romping, playing and joking with his children, all of whom adored him. The greatest pressure he faced in life was not leading troops, but in being away from his family. On the day before Christmas 1846, he tenderly wrote: 'I hope good Santa Claus will fill my Rob's stocking to-night: that Mildred's, Agnes's, and Anna's may break down with good things . . . but if he only leaves for you one half of what I wish, you will want for nothing.'

The demands of work may keep you from your family physically, but never let the pressures of work keep you from holding your children in your heart, and telling them they are there.

The man who fears no
truths has nothing
to fear from lies.

. . . may your love and your truth
always protect me.
Psalm 40:11 (NIV)

In his November 11, 1942 report on the war to the British House of Commons, Winston Churchill referred to 'the soft underbelly of the Axis'. On the surface, Hitler's regime seemed anything but soft. The powerful blitzkrieg of Nazi troops, the bravado and pageantry of the Third Reich seemed solidly powerful. What the British prime minister perceived, however, was the hidden side of the German dictator: his lack of character, his insecurity, his racially biased fears. He saw the moral darkness of his soul and predicted that when that darkness was exposed, it would create a black hole into which all of the Nazi claims would be sucked into oblivion.

Mark Twain used a similar word picture when he said, 'Everyone is a moon, and has a dark side which he never shows to anybody.'

When you face up to your own darkness of sin, you can either embrace it and pursue it – which leads to condemnation – or you can repent of sin and turn from it, trusting God to forgive you and flood your dark soul with light. In so doing, you ultimately find that you have no risk of exposure, because there's nothing to expose! You can't be truly embarrassed, because there's nothing you are desperate to hide.

Men will spend their
health getting wealth:
then gladly pay all
they have earned to
get health back.

*People who want to get rich fall into
temptation and a trap and into many
foolish and harmful desires that plunge
men into ruin and destruction.*
1 Timothy 6:9 (NIV)

Many people think that having money would solve all their problems. Consider the words of five of the wealthiest Americans in history:

John D. Rockefeller said, 'I have made many millions, but they have brought me no happiness. I would barter them all for the days I sat on an office stool in Cleveland and counted myself rich on three dollars a week.' Broken in health, despite his Christian beliefs, Rockefeller employed an armed guard in his latter years to ensure his personal safety.

W. H. Vanderbilt said, 'The care of 200 million dollars is too great a load for any brain or back to bear. It is enough to kill anyone. There is no pleasure in it.'

Wealthy businessman John Jacob Astor was a martyr to dyspepsia and melancholy who once said, 'I am the most miserable man on earth.'

Automobile king Henry Ford said, 'Work is the only pleasure . . . I was happier when doing a mechanic's job.'

Multimillionaire Andrew Carnegie once noted, 'Millionaires seldom smile.'

Money cannot satisfy the deep needs of the human heart. Learn to value your health because all the money in the world cannot buy it.

Many a man spanks his children for things his own father should have spanked him for.

Don't fail to correct your children; discipline won't hurt them! They won't die if you use a stick on them! Punishment will keep them out of hell.
Proverbs 23:13,14 (TLB)

Near the top of one of the highest peaks in the Rocky Mountain range – more than 10,000 feet above sea level – are two natural springs. They are so close together and level in height, that it would not take a great deal of effort to divert one streamlet towards the other. Yet, if you follow the course of one of these streams, you will find that it travels easterly and after traversing plateaus and valleys, receiving water from countless tributaries, it becomes part of the great Mississippi River and empties into the Gulf of Mexico.

If you follow the water from the other fountain, you will find that it descends gradually in a westerly direction, again combining with other tributaries until it becomes part of the Columbia River, which empties into the Pacific Ocean.

The terminal points of the two streams are more than five thousand miles apart, separated by one of the highest range of mountains in the world. And yet in their onset, the two streams are close neighbours. Very little effort would be required to make the easterly stream run west, or the westerly stream run east.

If you want to impact the course of a life . . . start at birth!

The first duty of love
is to listen.

Wherefore, my beloved brethren,
let every man be swift to hear.
James 1:19 (KJV)

Author and pastor's wife, Colleen Townsend Evans, has written, 'Silence need not be awkward or embarrassing, for to be with one you love, without the need for words, is a beautiful and satisfying form of communication.

'I remember times when our children used to come running to me, all of them chattering at once about the events of their day – and it was wonderful to have them share their feelings with me. But there were also the times when they came to me wanting only to be held, to have me stroke their heads and caress them into sleep. And so it is, sometimes, with us and with God our Father.'

Don't force your child to talk to you. Give him the respect and 'space' to remain silent. Sometimes children need to work out their own ideas and opinions in quiet before voicing them. On the other hand, when he does talk, take time to listen intently, carefully and kindly. In so doing, your child will know that he can talk to you whenever he wants or needs to, and you can rest assured that his silence is not rooted in suspicion or fear of you.

The language of silence *is* a language.

He that wants his son
to have respect for
him and his orders,
must himself have
a great reverence
for his son.

*Be devoted to one another in
brotherly love; give preference
to one another in honour.*
Romans 12:10 (NAS)

The parent who truly cares is a parent who will be available to give applause. Children take great delight in performing if they know their parents are in the audience and are present not solely for their own pleasure or enjoyment. This is even true for pre-schoolers.

A group of nursery school children was once overheard having this conversation:

Child 1: 'My daddy is a doctor and he makes lots of money and we have a swimming pool.'

Child 2: 'My daddy is a lawyer and he flies to Washington and talks to the President.'

Child 3: 'My daddy owns a company and we have our own airplane.'

Child 4 – to the envy of all the other children: 'My daddy is here!'

Children regard the public presence of their parents as a visible symbol of caring and connection that is far more important to them than any amount of material support. Be there for your child today. He'll remember your *presence* far more than your *presents*.

No person was ever
honoured for what he
received. Honour has
been the reward
for what he gave.

. . . the righteous gives and does not spare.
Proverbs 21:26 (NKJ)

He received two degrees, including a master of science degree. He was elected a fellow of the Society for the Encouragement of Arts, Manufactures, and Commerce in London and won the Spingarn Medal. He received a $100,000-a-year job offer from Thomas A. Edison. He received visits from Presidents Calvin Coolidge and Franklin Roosevelt, and an invitation from Joseph Stalin to superintend plantations in southern Russia. Yet for all he received, George Washington Carver is best known for what he gave.

He dedicated his life to making Tuskegee Institute an instrument of ministry to the needs of rural blacks – teaching them how to become skilled farmers and useful citizens. He taught better ways of tilling the soil, the importance of a balanced diet, and called upon black farmers to grow a variety of crops – including peanuts, sweet potatoes and cowpeas – instead of only cotton. He led the way towards the development of more than 300 derivative food and industrial products from peanuts, and more than 100 from sweet potatoes.

In the end, your résumé of accomplishments will mean little. Your gifts to others will count most!

Responsibility is the thing people dread most of all. Yet it is the one thing in the world that develops us, gives us manhood . . . fibre.

It will be good for that servant whom the master finds doing so when he returns.
Luke 12:43 (NIV)

One responsibility that we all have is the responsibility to do our best, which is to *strive* towards perfection. Consider the implications of people giving only a 99.9 per cent performance in these areas:

- Two million documents would be lost by the Internal Revenue Service this year.
- Twelve babies would be given to the wrong parents each day.
- Some 291 pacemaker operations would be performed incorrectly.
- Twenty thousand incorrect prescriptions would be written.
- Shoe manufacturers would ship out 114,500 mismatched pairs of shoes.

None of us will ever achieve perfection in all areas of our lives. But neither do any of us have an excuse for failing to try to do a 100-per cent job. As the owner of the Ritz Carlton Hotels said after his enterprise received the prestigious Malcolm Baldrige National Quality Award, 'Quality is a race with no finish line.'

'Giving it your best' means 'going for the top'.

We can either grace our children, or damn them with unrequited wounds which never seem to heal . . . men, as fathers you have such power!

The tongue has the power of life and death, and those who love it will eat its fruit.
Proverbs 18:21 (NIV)

A man once told this poignant story about his own conversion experience: 'My father was the senior elder in our church for many years. When I was a boy, eleven years of age, an evangelist held a series of meetings in our church. One night he asked every Christian to come forward and also asked those who desired to confess Christ to come with them. My father, of course, went up and, as I felt the call of God, I followed after him.

'Just as he reached the front he turned around and seeing me, said, "Johnnie, you go back; you are too young." I obeyed him, as I had been taught to do and at thirty-three I came again, but I did not know what I was coming for as clearly at thirty-three as I did at eleven.

'The church lost twenty-two years of service, while I lost twenty-two years of growth because my own father, an officer in the church, had said, "Go back." '

If you err at all, err on the side of your child knowing God, of his being old enough to experience God, and of his being mature enough to respond to God's offer of love and forgiveness.

Perhaps once in a hundred years a person may be ruined by excessive praise, but surely once every minute someone dies inside for a lack of it.

Do not let any unwholesome talk come out of your mouths, but only what is helpful for building others up according to their needs, that it may benefit those who listen.

Ephesians 4:29 (NIV)

Joan Benoit, the 1984 gold medalist in the first women's Olympic marathon, writes in her book, *Running Tide*:

'The neighbourhood beach association hired a lifeguard for the summer. He was also a Red Cross certified instructor in water safety; every summer he gave out certificates to kids who passed the Red Cross swimming tests.

'While I did not sink like a piece of lead in salt water, I was no great swimmer either. Every summer I was determined to show that lifeguard I could pass his tests, and every summer I failed. Every year the lifeguard watched me try once, then as much as said I should forget it. I think he believed I was hopeless. But I refused to be discouraged . . . His attitude made me so mad I vowed I would never give up. I kept working at it for the next three summers. Finally, when I was thirteen, I earned my Junior Lifesaving and Water Safety card.

'My feelings were hurt, not so much by the lifeguard as by my own limitations. I looked up to him because he was one of the best athletes my town had produced; I wanted to impress him and never did. He had no idea I was knocking myself out for a few kind words.'

To become a father
is not hard, to be
a father is, however.

*Get all the advice you can and
be wise the rest of your life.*
Proverbs 19:20 (TLB)

Your child makes you a father. As a father, you have the privilege not only of making your child, but of moulding and preparing your child for all eternity. No greater job description could ever be given to you!

Donald Grey Barnhouse has written a brief essay on 'Father and Son', in which he says:

> If a man begets a son, in consequence of that act, he is always the father of that son. There have been men who have been fathers of sons who have never been fathers *to* their sons. But many a man who begets a child, gives himself to that child. He is with the mother in the training of the child. The boy is with the father in his free moments. The father enters into the boy's studies; he participates in the boy's games. He makes the boy's hobbies his own hobbies. No question of the boy is beyond the patience of the father. He explains things to the child in great detail whenever the child shows interest in an answer. He trains the boy, leads him on, truly educates him. It can be said in the highest degree that this man is not only father *of* the boy, he is father *to* the boy.

Opportunities for meaningful communication between fathers and sons must be created. And it's work to achieve.

To every thing there is a season . . . a time to keep silence, and a time to speak.
Ecclesiastes 3:1,7b (KJV)

Most communication researchers and theorists contend that the first step in effective communication is 'gaining attention'. In order to establish lines of communication with your children, you first must 'attend' to them – really see them, really hear them, really listen to them, really feel what they feel.

The Hebrew word for *attend* has several meanings. Two of them paint vivid descriptions about the listening process:

• *a sharpened ear.* Such ears are like those of an animal listening to an unusual sound. Imagine a dog's ears being 'picked up' or 'perked up' to listen. That's the picture of a sharpened ear! As a father, you are challenged to tune in to your children, to listen to them with a heightened awareness.

• *a bent ear.* This is the ear that is 'cocked' in a certain direction – the ear positioned so that it hears fully and clearly, without distortion. As a father, put away anything that might distract you from listening to your child with your whole heart, mind and spirit. Bend your ear in your child's direction.

This type of active listening takes effort. It can be far more draining than talking. But it is also the foremost key to communicating with your child!

Big people
monopolise the
listening. Small
people monopolise
the talking.

*Do you see a man who is hasty
in his words? There is more hope
for a fool than for him.*
Proverbs 29:20 (RSV)

Shortly after President Franklin D. Roosevelt began his law practice as a young man in New York, he was retained to handle a very difficult and involved civil case. The opposing lawyer was a man of great experience who had a reputation for very effective closing statements to juries. Indeed, he completely outshone young Roosevelt in his arguments to the jury. He made one fatal mistake, however. His closing argument took several hours!

As the older and more experienced lawyer spoke on and on in his thunderous voice, Roosevelt noticed that the jury didn't seem to be paying much attention to him. So, playing a hunch when his turn came to speak, he rose and said: 'Gentlemen, you have heard the evidence. You also have listened to my distinguished colleague, a brilliant orator. If you believe him and disbelieve the evidence, you will have to decide in his favour. That's all I have to say.'

The jury was out for only five minutes before it brought in a verdict in favour of Roosevelt's client.

Those who speak at length tend to lose their audience.

Those who listen at length tend to gain a friend.

Don't be a lion in your own house.

*Not lording it over those
entrusted to you . . .*
1 Peter 5:3 (NIV)

A tyrannical husband once demanded that his wife conform to a rigid set of standards of his own choosing. She was to do certain things for him as a wife, keep house a certain way, dress a certain way, treat her children a certain way, speak and act in public a certain way She tried to please her husband, but over time, she came to hate his list of rules and regulations. Not surprisingly she soon grew to hate him. Then, one day the man died – an act of God's mercy, as far as the wife was concerned.

Some time later, she fell in love with another man and married him. To her surprise, she found that she and her new husband seemed to be on a perpetual honeymoon.

Joyfully, she devoted herself to his good welfare. One day while cleaning out some boxes in the attic, she came across one of the sheets of do's and don'ts her first husband had written for her to follow. To her amazement, she realized she was doing for her second husband all the things her first husband had demanded, even though her new husband had never once suggested them. She had been giving as an expression of love, not out of obedience to a demand.

Love and serve your wife . . . and you're likely to receive all the tender loving care you can receive!

Train your child in the
way in which you
know you should
have gone yourself.

*I will instruct you and teach you in
the way you should go; I will
counsel you and watch over you.*
Psalm 32:8 (NIV)

Most of us know of the Great Depression that occurred during the 1930s, but few know about the financial depression in the first half of the 1800s. Governments – from city to state to national – went into financial panic. Pennsylvania, one of the wealthier states at the time, repudiated its debts . . . in effect declaring itself insolvent. Illinois, then a fairly poor state, felt that with such a move made by its wealthy neighbour, it might be justified in doing likewise.

When Stephen Douglas heard of the proposal for repudiation, he opposed it strongly. Although he was very ill, he insisted that he be carried to the state legislature on a stretcher. Lying on his back he made this historic resolution:

'That Illinois be honest.' The motion touched the hearts of every member of the state house and the resolution was adopted with enthusiasm. The action by Illinois kept the practice of repudiation from spreading among the states. And many historians credit this move as a key reason Illinois is one of the most prosperous states today.

Taking the right road sometimes means taking the unpopular road with the highest toll. Teach your child that there is no substitute, however, for the rewards at the end of such a journey.

Attention Men: Before
you criticize another,
look closely at your
sister's brother.

*Do not judge others, so that God will
not judge you, for God will judge you
in the same way as you judge others,
and he will apply to you the same
rules you apply to others.*
Matthew 7:1,2 (GNB)

Willie had good cause to judge his father. His dad and mum had been teenage sweethearts and had married aged eighteen. But then his father abandoned his mother when she became pregnant and Willie didn't meet his father until nineteen years later.

He said, 'I was eager but nervous to meet my father. I didn't know what to expect. What I discovered was a kind, loving, sincere person, who actually cared for me. He and I talked for a long time. I began to understand his reasons for running away. I learned a lot about life and about myself from that conversation. I never held a grudge against my father . . .

'My father had his reasons for leaving. It wouldn't be fair to compare his life with mine. It would be like comparing baseball and football. I simply accepted my father as he was.

'I didn't offer judgment on what he had done, and I eventually grew to love him for what he was.'

Yes, Willie Stargell – an All-Star outfielder who played twenty years for the Pittsburgh Pirates – had good reason to criticize the father he never knew as a child . . . but he didn't.

You may think you have good cause to criticize another, but is it ever a good *enough* cause?

God sends no one
away except those
who are full
of themselves.

*God opposes the proud but
gives grace to the humble.*
1 Peter 5:5 (NIV)

In the last century, an American tourist heard that a renowned Polish rabbi, Hofetz Chaim, lived in the area where he was travelling. A great admirer of Rabbi Chaim, he asked if he might be able to visit him at his home. Word came back from the rabbi that he was welcome to stop by at any time.

The excited young tourist arrived at the rabbi's home and was invited to take off his knapsack and come inside. He entered the doorway to find only a simple one-room lodging. It was filled with books. The furnishings were limited to a table, a lamp and a bed.

The tourist asked in amazement, 'Rabbi, where is the rest of your furniture?' Hofetz Chaim replied, 'Where is yours?'

The puzzled American replied, glancing out of the door at his knapsack, 'My furniture? But I'm only a visitor here.' The rabbi responded, 'So am I.'

Very often it is when we empty ourselves not only of our pride, but of the possessions we pride ourselves in, that we truly can find those things which will last for all eternity. It is impossible to grasp hold of Heaven and earth with the same outstretched hand.

There is no more vital
calling or vocation for
men than fathering.

*So I run straight towards the goal in order
to win the prize, which is God's call
through Christ Jesus to the life above.*
Philippians 3:14 (GNB)

At the close of the sixteenth century, King Henry IV of France once was interrupted in his royal chamber by the Spanish ambassador. The envoy stood in astonishment at the sight he saw before him. There was the King of France on the floor, playing the part of horse while his young son rode on his back. Although the diplomat was speechless at the sight, the king was matter of fact. 'You are a father, too, Señor Ambassador,' he said, 'so we will finish our ride.'

While a significant part of fathering is to provide a role model for a child to 'look up to', an important aspect of fathering requires a man to get down on his child's level . . . indeed, to enter their world for play and exploration, and while there, to provide comfort, solace and assistance. The challenge is often not to be the 'big man' around the house, but to engage in the life of the 'little ones'. As Henry Ward Beecher once noted, 'Men cannot be developed perfectly who have not been compelled to bring children up to manhood. You might as well say that a tree is a perfect tree without leaf or blossom, as to say that a man is a man who has gone through life without experiencing the influences that come from bending down and giving one's self up to those who are helpless and little.'

The measure of a man
is not what he does
on Sunday but rather
who he is Monday
to Saturday.

*. . . that you may live a life worthy of the
Lord and may please him in every
way: bearing fruit in every good work.*
Colossians 1:10 (NIV)

In *Growing Wise in Family Life,* Charles R. Swindoll has written: 'You know what's helped us in the Swindoll home? To think of where we live as a training place, not a showplace. The home is a laboratory where experiments are tried out. It is a place where life makes up its mind. The home is a place where a child is free to think, to talk, to try out ideas. In a scene like that, God fits very comfortably into the entire conversation. And at any place where His name is inserted, it fits . . .

'Isn't that comfortable? Ready for a shocker? It's *supposed* to be comfortable! Christianity is designed for everyday living. Society has made it a "Sunday religion". But true-to-life Christianity is designed for Tuesday afternoon just as beautifully as Saturday morning or Sunday evening. Thank goodness, you don't have to dress up for it. It fits after a meal as well as before bedtime.'

Christianity is meant to be a spill-over religion – to fill up a person to *overflowing.* Our faith is meant to spill over into every day of the week, every action we take, every word we speak and every relationship we have. It's meant to spill over from our hearts to the hearts of others.

The world is blessed
most by men who
do things, and not
by those who merely
talk about them.

But be doers of the word, and not
hearers only, deceiving yourselves.
James 1:22 (RSV)

An old man once showed up at the back door of the house rented by a couple of university students. When they opened the door, they saw his eyes were glassy and his face unshaven. He bid them a good morning and then offered them some of the produce he was carrying in an old wicker basket. Although the produce was far from appealing, the students made a purchase, mostly to alleviate their pity and fear.

The visits became more regular. The students began to realize the glaze in his eyes was the result of cataracts, not alcohol. They became accustomed to his shuffling by, sometimes wearing mismatched shoes. He frequently punctuated his conversations by pulling out a harmonica to play gospel tunes.

On one visit he said, 'God is so good! I came out this morning and found a bag full of shoes and clothing on my doorstep.' The students rejoiced with him, 'We're happy for you!' Then he added, 'You know what's even more wonderful? Just yesterday I met some people who could really use 'em.'

No matter how little you may have or how little you know, you still have something you can *do* for both yourself and for others. As the old adage advises: talk only about the faith you live.

Authority without wisdom
is like a heavy axe
without an edge,
more fit to bruise
than polish.

. . . the authority the Lord gave me
for building you up, not for
tearing you down.
2 Corinthians 13:10 (NIV)

A number of years ago, an urgent and unusual invitation went out to a man to come quickly to a military academy. The students there had mutinied and the administrators hoped this particular man might help resolve the situation. The students were protesting against virtually everything: their classes, study hours, drill. The principal handed the mediator a large number of telegrams that had come from the parents of the boys involved. As he read through them, he felt as if he had been given a profile of the types of families from which the boys had come.

One father wired his son, 'I expect you to obey.' One said, 'If you are expelled from school, you needn't come home.' Another said, 'I'll send you to an asylum if you are sent home.' Yet another said, 'I'll cut you off without a shilling if you disgrace the family.'

In the final telegram, however, the mediator found the best message of the day, one from which he drew great hope. The message simply said, 'Steady, my boy, steady! Father.' 'At last,' noted the mediator, 'here is a man who believes in his son.'

There may very well be no greater influence upon a child than to have a father's respect, and to be treated in his or her teenage years as an adult.

Dad, when you come home at night with only shattered pieces of your dreams, your little one can mend them with two magic words – 'Hi, Dad!'

I myself have gained much joy and comfort from your love . . .
Philemon 7 (TLB)

Perhaps the most famous story told by Jesus is that of the Prodigal Son (Luke 15:11–24). The story is that of a young man who requests – and receives – his inheritance while his father is still alive. He takes his new wealth and squanders it, wasting it all in 'riotous living'. Penniless, he finds himself in a land of famine and ends up feeding swine and eating some of the husks meant for them just to keep his stomach full. No position could have been lower for a young Jewish man!

At that point the boy decides to return home, thinking only to request a position as a servant in his father's house. While he is still some distance from home, his father sees him, rises quickly and runs to greet him. The story could easily be retitled the parable of the Happy Father. The father not only kisses his son, but brings out the best robe and puts it on him. He places a ring on his finger and shoes on his feet, fully restoring him to sonship in the family. And then he orders a party in his son's honour.

No person can sadden or gladden the heart of a father like his son. You may know that feeling in your own life as a dad. But . . . does *your* father know it? Does your spiritual father? Does your Heavenly Father?

Unconditional love is loving a child no matter what . . . we expect him to be and, most difficult, no matter how he acts.

But show me unfailing kindness like that of the LORD as long as I live . . .
1 Samuel 20:14 (NIV)

A man visited his sister, the director of patient care for the children's unit of a large hospital, and as she gave him a tour through the unit, he heard the cries of a baby echoing through the halls. Finally, the man and his sister came to the child's room. He saw a one-year-old boy covered with terrible bruises, scratches and scars from head to toe.

The man assumed that the child must have been involved in a terrible accident. Then he looked closely at the little boy's legs. Written in ink all over them were obscenities. His sister explained that the child was a victim of parental abuse. His internal injuries were so severe that he couldn't keep down food. The scars on the bottom of the baby's feet were the result of cigarette burns.

The woman leaned over the baby's crib and carefully and tenderly lifted up the child and held him close to herself. At first the child screamed all the more, as if he expected to be hurt by human touch. But as she held the child securely, the baby relaxed in her arms and stopped crying. In spite of his wounds and hurts, he soaked up her tenderness like a sponge.

Hold your child close today and let him feel your heartbeat.

The value of marriage
is not that adults produce
children but that children
produce adults.

When I was a child, I spoke as a child,
I understood as a child, I thought as
a child; but when I became a man,
I put away childish things.
1 Corinthians 13:11 (NKJ)

Many people have thrilled to the voice of the opera star, Beverly Sills. Few know, however, that her natural daughter was born deaf and that she has a stepdaughter who is also severely handicapped.

She writes in her autobiography, *Bubbles*:

'I was now only thirty-four, but a very mature thirty-four. In a strange way my children had brought me an inner peace. The first question I had when I learned of their tragedies was self-pitying "Why me?" Then gradually it changed to a much more important "Why them?" Despite their handicaps they were showing enormous strength in continuing to live as normal and constructive lives as possible. How could Peter and I show any less strength?'

Oscar Wilde once wrote: 'In this world there are only two tragedies. One is not getting what one wants, and the other is getting it.' A third tragedy may be added: the tragedy of not being able to go forward after tragedy has occurred. When a tragedy strikes, our first tendency is to place blame on someone else. It is only when we are willing to accept our part of a tragedy that we truly make progress. It is from that position that we can ask God's forgiveness, and then forgive ourselves and move forward in our lives.

The best way to teach
character is to have it
around the house.

*The righteous man leads a blameless life;
blessed are his children after him.*
Proverbs 20:7 (NIV)

On the day before bass season opened, Jimmy and his father were fishing early in the evening on a New England lake. After using worms to catch perch and sunfish, Jimmy decided to practise casting with a small silver lure. No sooner had his lure hit the water than his pole doubled over. Jimmy knew right away that he had something huge on the line. By the time he reeled in the fish, a giant moon had risen over the lake. In the moonlight, Jimmy saw the biggest fish he had ever seen . . . but it was a bass.

Jimmy's dad lit a match to look at his watch: ten p.m. – two hours before bass season opened.

'You'll have to put it back, son,' he said. Jimmy protested, 'There'll never be another fish as big as this one!' He looked and saw no other fishermen or boats. Still, he knew by the tone of his father's voice that there would be no discussion. He carefully worked the hook from the lip of the bass and lowered it back into the water.

Jimmy was right. He takes his own children to that lake now and in the past thirty-four years, he never has seen a bass that big. But he readily admits that any time he faces a question of ethics, he sees that fish again and has to smile! A decision to do right always lives fresh and sweet in the memory.

The man who wins
may have been
counted out several
times, but he didn't
hear the referee.

*For though a righteous man falls seven
times, he rises again . . .*
Proverbs 24:16 (NIV)

After Dwight Eisenhower won the Republican nomination for President from Robert Taft in 1952, a reporter asked Taft about his goals. He replied, 'My great goal was to become President of the United States in 1953.'

The reporter smirked and said, 'Well, you didn't make it, did you?'

Taft responded, 'No, but I became senator from Ohio!'

Imagine a target of the type used for playing darts. The bull's-eye is usually marked for one hundred points. Concentric rings are labelled 80, 60, 40, 20. Bull's-eye scores are rare; players often hit lesser-valued rings. But nearly every dart player will tell you that if he doesn't *aim* for the bull's-eye, he scores lower than he would otherwise. And the person who doesn't aim and throw at all, scores zero!

Someone once said, 'I would rather attempt to do something great for God and fail, than do nothing and succeed.' Another has said, 'Shoot for the moon. Even if you don't make it, you'll land among the stars.'

Keep company with good
men and good men
you will imitate.

As iron sharpens iron, so one man
sharpens another.
Proverbs 27:17 (NIV)

Our friends and associations during our youth are like a prophecy of our future character and destiny.

Voltaire's agnosticism has been traced by some to the Abbé de Chateuneuf, who, although a priest, sowed the seeds of deism in Voltaire. One can only imagine that with a different environment in his youth, Voltaire might have been just as powerful a voice for the faith as he became for unbelief.

The English philosopher, John Locke, on the other hand, had Lord Somers as a friend and counsellor during his youth. Somers has been described as 'one of those divine men who, like a chapel in a palace, remains unprofaned, while all the rest is tyranny corruption and folly'. He left his mark on Locke.

John Wesley, while at Oxford, determined to have no friends other than those who could help him in the life of faith he was trying to lead.

Help your child choose his or her friends wisely. And on your child's behalf, choose wise teachers, mentors and counsellors. The choice of your child's influencers may be among the greatest choices you ever make as a father.

The great man is he
who does not lose
his child's heart.

*And he shall turn the heart of the fathers
to the children, and the heart of the
children to their fathers . . .*
Malachi 4:6 (KJV)

A little boy named Jay Rial loved the sound of the train whistle that brought the circus to town. He loved the circus band, the clowns, the animals. He loved the performers and the very tent itself. He loved the smell of peanuts, the roar of the lions and the beautiful ladies who rode the beautiful horses. Once he was allowed to stand in the middle of the sawdust-covered ring when they were preparing the tent. It was a great moment for him! Little Jay Rial vowed, 'If I ever get to be a big man, I'm going to take just as many children to the circus with me as I can.' He called it his circus dream.

It was a dream he remembered. As an adult, Jay Rial went into the circus business as an 'advance man'. Each year when the circus came to the biggest city on its tour, Jay Rial arranged for every child in every hospital and orphanage – as well as any child who was handicapped or not as fortunate as other children – to come to the circus free. When more children showed up than the tent could hold, Jay Rial didn't turn them away, he arranged for *another* circus party!

Jay Rial's childhood dream came true. And in the process, he also made dreams come true for countless children.

An ounce of loving role modelling is worth a pound of parental pressure.

*In everything set them an example
by doing what is good.*
Titus 2:7 (NIV)

A boy lost his left arm at the shoulder when he was only seven years old. Until he was twelve, he cried himself to sleep every night. He found it impossible to see the amputation as ever having any good outcome. Gradually, however, he began to conquer his handicap. By tucking a long-handled hoe under his armpit, he soon learned to hoe as many rows as his brothers.

Later in life, he sold life insurance, and was very successful at it. He learned to play handball and at one time, held the national championship in that sport. He also became adept at golf, hunting and fishing.

One day he learned of a thirteen-year-old boy who had gone through a similar amputation. The boy had no will to live and his condition was worsening. The man took his scrapbook and went to the hospital to see the boy. Nothing was said about the arm, but as the boy looked at the various newspaper clippings he finally asked, 'Is this you?' The man removed his shirt and showed the boy his armless shoulder.

The boy sighed deeply and soon fell asleep. Three days later he was on the mend and soon after, he left the hospital.

You are the first and foremost role model your child will have. What you 'show' to your child will be vastly more influential than what you 'tell' your child.

Every child comes
with the message
that God is not yet
discouraged of man.

*. . . what is man that you are mindful
of him, the son of man that you care for
him? You made him a little lower
than the heavenly beings and crowned
him with glory and honour.*
Psalm 8:4,5 (NIV)

A little shepherd boy was watching his sheep one Sunday morning. As he heard the bells ringing the faithful to church, and watched the people walking to church along the lane next to the pasture, he began to think that he, too, would like to communicate with God. *But what can I say?* he thought. He had never learned a prayer. So, on bended knee, he began to recite the alphabet – A, B, C, D and so on to Z, repeating his 'prayer' several times.

A man passing by heard the boy's voice and looking through the bushes, he saw the young man kneeling with folded hands, closed eyes, saying, 'J, K, L, M . . .' He interrupted the boy, asking, 'What are you doing, my little friend?' The boy replied, 'I was praying, sir.' The man seemed surprised and said, 'But why are you reciting the alphabet?'

The boy explained, 'I don't know any prayers, sir. But I want God to take care of me and help me to care for the sheep. So, I thought if I said all I knew, He could put the letters together into words and spell all that I want and should say.' The man smiled and said, 'Bless your heart. You're right. God will!' and went on to church, knowing he had already heard the finest sermon he could possibly hear that day.

My father is the
standard by which
all subsequent men
in my life have
been judged.

*. . . leaving us an example, that you
should follow His steps.*
1 Peter 2:21 (NKJ)

Two million dollars to the Cité Universitaire in France, the restoration of Rheims Cathedral, the repair of palaces at Versailles and Fontainebleau, $500,000 for the Shakespeare Memorial Theatre at Stratford-on-Avon, $4 million for Acadia National Park, $500,000 for Jewish farm development in Russia, 54 acres for a New York City park, $3.5 million to the New York Public Library . . . the list goes on and on! Most of the gifts are credited to John D. Rockefeller, but it was his son who made the decisions about how to distribute the money accumulated by his father. Shortly before his father's 94th birthday, J. D. Rockefeller, Jr., wrote to his father:

'I have tried to do what I thought you would have me do . . . I have endeavored to use wisely and unselfishly the means that you have so unselfishly placed at my disposal . . . In all these years of effort and striving, your own life and example have ever been to me the most powerful and stimulating influence. What you have done for humanity and business on a vast scale has impressed me profoundly. To have been a silent partner with you in carrying out these great constructive purposes and benefactions has been the supreme delight of my life.'

Some parents bring
up their children
on thunder and
lightning, but thunder
and lightning never yet
made anything grow

. . . you should practise tenderhearted
mercy and kindness to others . . . Most
of all, let love guide your life . . .
Colossians 3:12,14 (TLB)

A family once planned a month's vacation to the West Coast of America. At the last minute, the father was unable to go because of work responsibilities. Mum insisted she was capable of driving and she and the children went ahead with their trip. Dad helped plan their route and arranged where they would stop each night.

As it turned out, Dad was able to complete his work within two weeks. He decided to surprise the family so he flew to a West Coast city without calling them. Then he took a taxi out of the city and asked to be let off along the road on which, according to his travel plan, the family should be driving later that day. When he saw the family car, he stuck out his thumb like a hitchhiker. As Mum and the children drove past, they did a double-take. One of the children exclaimed, 'Mum, wasn't that Dad!' The car came to a screeching stop and the family enjoyed a joyful reunion.

When a reporter later asked the man why he did such a crazy thing, he said, 'After I die, I want my kids to be able to say, "Dad sure was fun, wasn't he?"'

Laughter and fun times are like gentle rain on your child's personality. Not only do they cause your child to flourish, but they enable the fertilizer of guidance and discipline to soak in.

My Dad and I hunted and fished together. How could I get angry at this man who took the time to be with me?

Honour thy father . . .
Exodus 20:12 (KJV)

During war games, Private Glenn Sollie and Private Andrew Bearshield of the Fifteenth Infantry were ordered to make their way to a bridge and stand guard there until they were relieved.

The two were faithful soldiers. They went to the bridge and guarded it . . . and guarded it. They stuck to their job for three days and nights, with neither food nor blankets. They eventually were found rather than 'relieved'. The two privates had been guarding the wrong bridge! They had lost their way and taken their battle stations at a bridge seven miles away from the one they were to guard. One might suppose they were reprimanded for making such a mistake. On the contrary, they were given military honours for guarding their position with such faithfulness!

Very often our parents make mistakes in life. They can make 'wrong turns' or follow what turn out to be foolish pursuits. But rather than criticize them or blame them for their errors, we can choose to focus on what they did right! In turning our attention to their positive qualities and deeds – however meagre they may be – we usually find we have no difficulty giving them 'honour'.

Unless a father
accepts his faults he
will most certainly
doubt his virtues.

. . . He made us accepted in the Beloved.
Ephesians 1:6 (NKJ)

A father lost his temper one morning in one of those 'irritating situations' that tend to happen in life. He unleashed his frustration and anger on his son, who happened to be the closest 'target'. Later in the day, while he and his son were fishing, he became convicted about what he had said and done. He began, 'Son, I was a little impatient this morning.'

'Uh huh,' the son grunted, reeling in his line and preparing to cast again. The father continued, 'Uh . . . I realize I was a little hard to be around.'

Again, 'Uh huh,' was the only response his son made.

The father continued, 'I – I want you to know that, uh, I feel bad about it.' Then, quick to justify himself, he added, 'But you know, son, there are times that I'm like that.' The boy merely said, 'Uh huh.'

A few seconds passed, and then the boy added, 'You know, Dad, God uses you to teach all of us in the family patience.'

Our families have a way of 'nailing us' with their honesty, but rather than feeling hammered, take what they say as good advice. Nobody else can help you grow into the nature of Christ Jesus as much as your family members can!

What was silent in the
father speaks in the son,
and often I have found the
son the unveiled secret
of the father.

And he did that which was right
in the sight of the LORD . . .
as Joash his father did.
2 Kings 14:3 (KJV)

While a man was awaiting surgery in a hospital, he began talking with his father. 'I really hope I can be home by Father's Day,' he said. The two talked of various Father's Day celebrations they had shared through the years and then the son said wistfully, 'I still feel awful that when I was ten years old, I didn't give you either a card or a gift.'

The father replied, 'Son, I remember the Saturday before that Father's Day I saw you in a shop although you didn't see me. I watched as you picked up several cigars and stuffed them in your pocket. I knew you had no money and I suspected you were about to steal those cigars as a present for me. I felt extremely sad to think you would leave the store without paying for them. But almost as soon as you tucked the cigars in your pocket, you pulled them out and put them back in the box on the shelf.

'When you stayed out playing all the next day because you had no present to give me, you probably thought I was hurt. You were wrong. When you put those cigars back and decided not to break the law, you gave me the best Father's Day present I ever received.'

Gentlemen, try not
to become men
of success.
Rather, become
men of value.

The righteous man walks in his integrity.
Proverbs 20:7 (NKJ)

Charles Lindbergh, although a celebrity who achieved international fame, remained an enigma to many people. Few could understand why he did not seek to capitalize more on his historic flight across the Atlantic in 1927. Commercializing the flight seemed to be the last thing Lindbergh wanted to do.

One person estimated that Lindbergh could have made five million dollars in one week if he had accepted the hundreds of offers he received to sign testimonials, write books or go into movies. William Randolph Hearst alone offered him half a million dollars to star in a film about aviation. He was offered a vaudeville contract with a one-million-dollar guarantee. A movie company made him a million-dollar offer and another movie company upped its offer to five million. All were turned down. Others sent money to Lindbergh as gifts. All of it was returned.

An associate of Lindbergh summed up Lindbergh's perspective on these many ways he might have added fortune to his fame. He said simply, 'Lindbergh won't take money he hasn't earned.'

The money one gains in life counts for little if it isn't *earned* legally and morally, and if it isn't *spent* in accordance with sound values.

A man's children
and his garden both
reflect the amount of
weeding done during
the growing season.

*He who withholds his rod hates
his son, but he who loves him
disciplines him diligently.*
Proverbs 13:24 (NAS)

Pastor Stephen Bly writes in *How to Be a Good Dad:*
'When we first moved to northern Idaho, our front yard consisted of nothing but weeds. Sooner or later, we had to tackle the yard. Mike, at fifteen, seemed a likely prospect to handle the job. But about five minutes after starting, he came back into the house. "I need some gloves," he reported . . . he spent twenty minutes looking for gloves. After a brief time back in the yard, he returned again. "I've got to have some music . . ." He spent fifteen minutes setting up his portable stereo . . . Ten minutes later I saw him again. "It's hot out there. I've got to have a drink." Finally, I thought I heard him chopping. But not for long . . . "Hey, Dad," he said, "you know what we need? . . . If we had one of those electric weed whips . . ."

' "Mike!" I began in my best drill sergeant's voice, "I don't care if it takes you all day, all week, or all month. You and that hoe are going to chop down every weed. Then you're going to rake them and carry them off. Now, stop stalling." '

Bly concludes, 'I'm sure I sounded insensitive . . . but I did care. I cared enough to know that Mike, like all of us, needed to learn to put in a hard day's work. Caring dads teach good work habits.'

If it is desirable that children be kind, appreciative and pleasant, then those qualities should be taught – not hoped for.

For these commands are a lamp, this teaching is a light, and the corrections of discipline are the way to life.

Proverbs 6:23 (NIV)

A king once decided to honour the greatest of his subjects. Word went throughout the kingdom and various recommendations were immediately forthcoming. A man of wealth and property was singled out. One person was lauded for her healing skills, another for his fair practice of the law. Still another was praised for his honesty in business and yet another for his bravery as a soldier. Each candidate for the title of 'greatest' was brought to the palace and presented to the king. He admitted to his counsellors that this choice was going to be very difficult.

As the last day before the honour ceremony arrived, the last candidate was finally brought before the king – a white-haired woman whose eyes sparkled with the light of knowledge, love and understanding.

'Who is this?' the king asked. 'What has she accomplished of note?' An aide replied, 'You have seen and heard all the other candidates. This woman is their teacher.' Those in the court erupted into applause and the king immediately stepped from his throne to honour her.

Virtues do not happen by accident or as a natural part of growth. As with any skill or means of success, they must be taught.

Our children give us
the opportunity
to become the
parents we always
wish we had.

*Do for others what you want
them to do for you . . .*
Matthew 7:12 (GNB)

Encounter once published this list of 'Ten Things for Which You as a Parent Will Never Be Sorry':

1. For doing your level best even when discouraged.
2. For hearing before judging in family quarrels.
3. For thinking before speaking when emotionally upset.
4. For not harbouring unkind thoughts of a talebearer.
5. For being generous to an enemy, perhaps the next-door neighbour.
6. For stopping your ears to gossip over the fence.
7. For standing by your principles in dealing with your teenagers.
8. For asking pardon, when in error, even of your child.
9. For being square in business dealings with the newspaper boy.
10. For accepting the stewardship of 'another' child.

Most of us know the ideals of being a good parent. Putting those ideals into practice is what's hard – but also what is most rewarding!

To be successful in the family the father must have the welfare of each family member at heart and his decisions and plans must be based upon what is best for them.

Do nothing from selfishness or empty conceit, but with humility of mind regard one another as more important than yourselves
Philippians 2:3 (NAS)

A twelve-year-old girl named Susan hated having to share a bedroom with her seven-year-old sister. She dreamed of being an only child with a room all of her own. Apparently her father seemed to have the same idea. He was attending night school and longed for a room where he could study in quiet, away from his noisy family. He decided to build such a room for himself. Throughout the summer months, he poured the foundation, hammered, sawed and installed wiring and windows. Although work slowed during the autumn months, the heat was finally connected, the carpet laid and the built-in bookshelf completed.

On the last day before the Christmas holiday, Susan came home from school to find the bedroom she shared with her sister completely rearranged. Angry with her sister for having upset the room, she raced down the hall after her into the new addition to the house. There, her parents greeted her with a shout of 'Surprise!' To Susan's amazement, she found that all her possessions had been moved, her clothes hung in the closet, her books placed on the shelves.

'Daddy knew you needed your own room,' her mother said, 'so he decided you should have this one.'

Children miss nothing in sizing up their parents. If you are only half convinced of your beliefs, they will quickly discern that fact.

Let us hold fast the profession of our faith without . . .
Hebrews 10:23 (KJV)

Karl, a young Jewish boy in Germany had a profound sense of admiration for his father. The life of the family centred around the acts of piety and devotion prescribed by their religion. The father was zealous in attending worship and instruction, and demanded the same from his children. When Karl was just a teenager, the family moved. Their new town had no synagogue. To Karl's surprise, his father announced to the family that they were going to abandon their Jewish traditions and join the Lutheran church. He explained that this was necessary to help his business, since the leading citizens of the town were Lutheran.

Karl was both disappointed and confused by this action. His bewilderment gave way to anger and an intense bitterness that remained within him throughout his life. He left Germany and went to England to study. While there, he conceived of a movement that he hoped would change the entire world, and he wrote a manuscript of his ideas. In his book he termed religion as an 'opiate for the masses' that could be explained in strictly economic terms. Billions of people eventually came to live under the government system conceived by Karl Marx – it was called communism.

Children are our most valuable natural resource.

Children are an heritage of the L‍ORD . . .
Psalm 127:3 (KJV)

Martin Luther had a reputation as an excellent father who used just the right way of discipline and love. He believed: 'Punish if you must, but let the sugar plum go with the rod.' He composed songs for his children, playing his lute while his children sang them. His letters to his children are jewels.

Luther especially had a tender place in his heart for his daughter Magdalena, about whom he said, 'God has given no bishop so great a gift in a thousand years as He has given me in her.' When she became ill at the age of fourteen, he prayed constantly for her, finally praying, 'I love her very much, but, dear God, if it is Thy holy will to take her, I would gladly leave her with Thee.' To Lena he said, 'Dear, my little daughter, thou wouldst love to remain here with thy father; art thou willing to go to that other Father?' His daughter said, 'Yes, dear father, just as God wills.' When she died, he wept long and as she was laid in the earth he spoke to her as to a living soul: 'You will rise and shine like the stars and the sun.'

Most of us think of natural resources and riches as coming from the earth. May none of us have to lay a precious child into the earth to realize too late that our child has been far more valuable to us than earth's riches.

A young branch takes
on all the bends that
one gives to it.

*Train up a child in the way
he should go: and when he is old,
he will not depart from it.*
Proverbs 22:6 (KJV)

Stan's father was manager of a road construction company. One day when Stan was about ten years old, he went with his father to the shop. Paving materials were stockpiled there, including a pile of rock. Being a cricketer, Stan felt compelled to throw a few of those rocks while his father went inside the shop. Unfortunately one of the rocks put a big spiderweb crack in the windshield of his dad's car!

No one was around and Stan's first thought was to blame the crack on the gang of kids who customarily passed the shop about that time each day. Still, Stan wasn't comfortable with a lie. When his father returned to the car, Stan was there waiting. With tears in his eyes, he told his father what had happened, fully expecting to be punished soundly. His father surprised him, however, by calling the incident an accident. He noted that Stan could have blamed others, and he admired his honesty. And then, he told his son that since he felt it was right for Stan to pay part of the damages, he would be forced to adjust Stan's weekly allowance – which he did – from 25 pence a week up to 50 pence a week so he could pay 25 pence a week towards the new windshield!

If there be any truer
measure of a man than
by what he does, it must
be by what he gives.

It is more blessed to give than to receive.
Acts 20:35 (KJV)

I

At a church meeting a very wealthy man rose to give a testimony. 'I'm a millionaire,' he said, not at all humbly. 'I attribute it all to the rich blessings of God in my life. I came from a wonderful family. He gave me abundant intelligence and good business sense. I worked hard. On the night after I received my first paycheck, I went to a church meeting. The speaker was a missionary who told about his work. I gave everything I had to God. I believe that God blessed that decision, and that is why I am a rich man today.'

After smiling broadly at the congregation, he sat down. After a few seconds of silence in the church, a tiny elderly woman sitting in the pew behind him leaned forward and said, 'I dare you to do it again.'

Pride in self is the very antithesis of a good heart. As a missionary discovered when he attempted to translate the word 'pride' for a tribe noted for its common sharing, pride can be a difficult concept to define. Yet, it is one universally recognized. The missionary finally attached an air pump to a bicycle tyre and, while pointing first to one head and then to another, began to pump hard until the tyre inflated to several times its size . . . and burst. Everyone in the village nodded in understanding!

Men for the sake
of getting a living
forget to live.

*It is vain for you to rise up early,
to take rest late, to eat the bread of
(anxious) toil – for He gives
(blessings) to His beloved in sleep.*
Psalm 127:2 (AMP)

At a Rotary meeting in Illinois a number of years ago, Gypsy Smith gave a stirring speech to the leading business and professional men of the city. As he prepared to close his remarks, he lifted his well-worn Bible high above his head and then asked the men there, 'How many of you men can recall a saintly mother and a godly father who loved this Book, read it, lived it and seeped it into you?'

Nearly every man in the room, with moist eyes and sober expression, raised a hand.

Then quietly and deftly Gypsy made his final statement. 'With all your influence today how many of you are so living that your children will remember you for your faithfulness to this same Book?'

It was a tense moment. The point had sunk deep into the hearts of those in attendance, bringing conviction and a silence in which one might hear a pin drop. Not a hand was raised.

If you were asked these two questions today how would you answer them?

In all of our 'earning' a living, may we never forget the joy of the life we have already been *given* as a gift and a godly heritage.

If a man cannot be
a Christian in the
place where he is,
he cannot be a
Christian anywhere.

Let your light so shine before men, that
they may see your good works, and glorify
your Father which is in heaven.
Matthew 5:16 (KJV)

Fifteen-year-old Heidi doubled over with stomach pains while backpacking. After being rushed to the hospital and undergoing surgery to stop her internal bleeding, Heidi seemed to recover quickly. Then tests revealed an adrenal tumour. Heidi underwent more surgery, followed by extensive radiation. She asked her father, 'Why me, Dad?' Her father answered, 'Honey, the book of Matthew says, "Ye are the light of the world . . . Let your light so shine before men, that they may see your good works, and glorify your Father which is in heaven." I know you have accepted Jesus as your personal Saviour and have become one of His lights, sweetheart.'

Two years later, Paul watched his 'light', Heidi, receive her high-school diploma, and then the cancer struck again, this time in her lungs. As Paul embraced his daughter, he could say only, 'Honey all we can do is call on the Lord for His strength.' Another surgery followed. And the following Christmas Paul again witnessed joy as his 'light', Heidi, married. The following April, Heidi died as a result of brain cancer.

How hard it is for a father to be a Christian when his daughter is suffering and dying! Paul saw Heidi as one of God's 'lights', but surely he was also a light to her in her greatest hours of need.

You cannot live a perfect day without doing something for someone who will never be able to repay you.

And do not forget to do good and to share with others, for with such sacrifices God is pleased.
Hebrews 13:16 (NIV)

When Frank arrived at the Pearly Gates, he very quickly found himself standing face to face with an impressive angelic being holding a clipboard. The angel told Frank he needed to get some 'entry data' – name, address, a few other particulars. As part of the form completion, the angel said, 'Frank, it would help if you could identify one experience from your life on earth in which you did a purely unselfish, kind deed.'

Frank thought for a few seconds and then said, 'Well, I think I have something that qualifies. One day as I was walking, I came upon a little old lady who was being beaten mercilessly by a rough motorbike gang member. He was smacking her around so I stepped right up and pushed over his motorbike – but only to distract him. Then I kicked him real hard in the shins and shouted for the old lady to run for help. Then I hauled off and put my fist right into the guy's stomach. I think the old lady made it to safety.'

'Wow,' the angel replied, 'that is very impressive.' Then, with pen poised on his clipboard, he asked, 'When did this happen?' Frank looked at his watch and replied, 'Oh, two or three minutes ago.'

Make today a perfect day by doing something for someone who can never repay you!

From good parents come a good son.

A good tree cannot bear bad fruit . . .
Matthew 7:18 (NIV)

During his tenure as president of Princeton University, Woodrow Wilson was once asked to speak to a parents' group. He said, in part: 'I get many letters from you parents about your children. You want to know why we people up here in Princeton can't make more out of them and do more for them. Let me tell you the reason we can't. It may shock you just a little, but I am not trying to be rude. The reason is that they are your sons, reared in your homes, blood of your blood, bone of your bone. They have absorbed the ideals of your homes. You have formed and fashioned them. They are your sons. In those malleable, mouldable years of their lives you have forever left your imprint upon them.'

While most parents hope their children will enjoy a higher standard of living than they themselves have experienced, what many parents fail to realize is that a child will rarely exhibit a higher standard of morality, ambition and godliness than that which his parents displayed. We can never expect a teacher, pastor, mentor, counsellor, friend or Sunday school teacher to impart to our children that which only we as parents can give and do. You are the main 'star' in your child's life. All others are supporting actors.

Among all the abuses
of the world . . . there
is none worse than
a negligent father.

*But you have neglected the more
important matters of the law –
justice, mercy and faithfulness.*
Matthew 23:23c (NIV)

After several months in a therapy group, Stuart decided to visit his twenty-year-old son at college. He asked the boy what it had been like to have him as a father. 'Well, Dad,' he said, 'I don't want to hurt your feelings . . . but you were never there.'

'What do you mean?' Stuart asked. 'I was there every evening. I never went anywhere!' The boy said, 'I know, Dad, but it was like there was nothing to you. You never got mad. If you were ever sad, I never knew it. You never seemed happy . . . I didn't know who you were. You were like a stranger to me . . . most of the time I felt like I didn't have a father.'

In relating this back to his therapy group, Stuart broke down and cried for the first time in more than forty years. 'Can you believe it?' he asked. 'I was there . . . and he felt I was invisible.'

Eventually Stuart got past his dismay and went through a real emotional growth surge. He joined an outdoor club and took his son white-water rafting and deep-sea fishing. One night he told the group, 'I'm so angry. So much of my life has been wasted. And what I really regret is that I've hurt my son – not because I ever did anything mean, but because there was so little inside of me for him to see.'

It is never too late. Let your child see 'inside' of you.

Children need love, especially when they do not deserve it.

Therefore be imitators of God,
as beloved children; and walk in love,
just as Christ also loved you and gave
Himself up for us, an offering and a
sacrifice to God as a fragrant aroma.
Ephesians 5:1,2 (NAS)

A shepherd once had a sheep that ate from his hand and followed him everywhere. When he was asked to explain the close relationship, the shepherd smiled and replied that this particular sheep had once been the most wayward in his flock.

In its first year of life, the sheep had wandered away numerous times, costing the shepherd many long hours of searching. Finally the shepherd broke the lamb's leg. He then bound the leg in a splint and carried the sheep with him to the hills. There, he fed it by hand and brought it water to drink. Day by day he took care of the lamb until it had fully recovered.

After that, the sheep never went astray again. In fact, it followed the shepherd more closely than a dog might follow its master.

Expressions of love to a child very often involve discipline coupled with closeness of caring. When a child errs and strays from what is right, it is then that a parent must show love in extraordinary ways – coupling any disciplinary action with tenderness and closeness. The purpose of such discipline must always be like that of the Great Shepherd, who 'restoreth' our souls.

Praise your children
openly, reprove
them secretly.

*Discipline your son, and he will give you
rest; he will give delight to your heart.*
Proverbs 29:17 (RSV)

Young Teddy once listened as his father told, at great length and in great detail, about a time in the past when Teddy showed great wisdom and poise under fire. The child kept tugging at his dad's trouser leg all the while he was talking. The father, annoyed, finally leaned over to see what his son wanted. 'Dad,' the child whispered loudly. 'That wasn't me. It was Billy!' Embarrassed before his friend, the father took Teddy by the arm and marched him to the woodshed.

All the way there, Teddy kept saying, 'Dad, Dad.' The father, at his wit's end, stopped and said, 'Now what? I suppose you're going to tell me that Billy is the one who openly ridiculed me in front of my friend?'

'No,' said the boy, 'I'm hoping that when you see your friend tomorrow you can brag about how you didn't punish me even when you wanted to.'

Whether praising or correcting your child, make sure you are telling the truth! Open and truthful praise before others builds up your child . . . but lies or false flattery creates false self-esteem. Secret correction spares your child humiliation and retains your child's dignity and self-respect. But reproof that is unfounded or rooted in falsehood can cause great damage, even if spoken behind closed doors.

Every man is
enthusiastic at times.
One man has
enthusiasm for thirty
minutes, another has it
for thirty days – but it
is the man that has it
for thirty years who
makes a success in life.

*. . . let us run with perseverance
the race marked out for us.*
Hebrews 12:1 (NIV)

Three ditch diggers were on the job one day. An observer watched as one man leaned on his shovel and began to brag about how he was going to be a foreman in the ditch-digging company some day. The second man then stopped to lean on his shovel as he began to complain about the long hours, the hard work and the low pay. The third man just kept digging.

Years went by. The observer came across a ditch-digging crew in the same area and asked about the three men he had seen years before. To his surprise, one of the men stopped digging, leaned on his shovel, and said, 'Why, I was one of those men.' He was still leaning on his shovel!

'And your friends?' the observer asked.

'Oh,' said the man, 'ol' Sam was always complaining about this and that, and one day he just up and said he was injured. Don't know what happened . . . but he's been on disability ever since.'

'And the third man?'

The ditch digger replied, 'Why he owns the whole company now.'

Measure wealth not
by the things you have,
but by the things you
have for which you
would not take money.

*. . . a man's life does not consist in
the abundance of his possessions.*
Luke 12:15 (NIV)

During the Depression, many families could scarcely afford the bare essentials, much less buy presents at Christmas. 'But, I'll tell you what we can do,' said the father to his six-year-old son, Pete. 'We can use our imaginations and make pictures of the presents we would like to give each other.'

For the next few days, each member of the family worked secretly but with joy. On Christmas morning, huddled around a scraggly tree decorated with pitifully few decorations, the family gathered to exchange the presents they had created. And what gifts they were! Daddy got a shiny black limousine and a red motor boat. Mum received a diamond bracelet and a new hat. Little Pete had fun opening his gifts, a drawing of a swimming pool and pictures of toys cut from magazines.

Then it was Pete's turn to give his present to his parents. With great delight, he handed them a brightly coloured crayon drawing of three people – man, woman and little boy. They had their arms around one another and under the picture was one word: us. Even though other Christmases were far more prosperous for this family no Christmas in their memory stands out as more precious!

It takes time
to be a good father.
It takes effort –
trying, failing
and trying again.

*And let us not get tired of doing what is
right, for after a while we will reap a
harvest of blessing if we don't get
discouraged and give up.*
Galatians 6:9 (TLB)

While at the park one day a woman sat down next to a man on a bench near a playground. 'That's my son over there,' she said, pointing to a little boy in a red sweater who was gliding down the slide. 'He's a fine looking boy,' the man said. 'That's my son on the swing in the blue sweater.' Then, looking at his watch, he called to his son, 'What do you say we go, Sam?'

Sam pleaded, 'Just five more minutes, Dad. Please? Just five more minutes.' The man nodded and Sam continued to swing to his heart's content.

Minutes passed and the father stood and called again to his son, 'Time to go now?' Again Sam pleaded, 'Five more minutes, Dad. Just five more minutes.' The man smiled and said, 'OK.'

'My, you certainly are a patient father,' the woman said.

The man smiled and then said, 'My older son Tommy was killed by a drunk driver last year while he was riding his bike near here. I never spent much time with him and now I'd give anything for just five more minutes with him. I've vowed not to make the same mistake with Sam. He thinks he has five more minutes to swing. The truth is, I get five more minutes to watch him play.'

Children desperately
need to know – and
to hear in ways they
understand and
remember –
that they're loved
and valued
by Mum and Dad.

*. . . let us stop just saying we love
people; let us really love them,
and show it by our actions.*
1 John 3:18 (TLB)

Lee Iacocca, former president of Ford Motor Company and former CEO of Chrysler Corporation, writes in his book, *Straight Talk:*

'My parents spent a lot of time with me, and I wanted my kids to be treated with as much love and care as I got. Well, that's a noble objective . . . but to translate it into daily life, you really have to work at it.

'I spent all my weekends with the kids and all my vacations. Kathi was on the swim team for seven years, and I never missed a meet. Then there were tennis matches . . . and piano recitals. I made all of them too. I was always afraid that if I missed one, Kathi might finish first or finish last and I would . . . not be there to congratulate – or console – her.

'The same with Lia . . . Once I picked up Lia at Brownie camp. She was six years old and came running out to the car in her new khaki uniform with an orange bandana around her neck and a little beanie on her head. She had just made it into the Potawatami Tribe. She had hoped to join the Nava-joes, as she called them, but she was turned down. Still, she was excited, and so was I. Funny thing, I missed an important meeting that day but for the life of me I have no recollection of what it was.'

Happiness is inward
and not outward;
and so, it does not
depend on what we have,
but on what we are.

*Beware! Don't always be wishing for what
you don't have. For real life and real
living are not related to how rich we are.*
Luke 12:15 (TLB)

An old legend tells of a tribe that was continually at war with other tribes. This violent tribe murdered, raped and pillaged their neighbours. They appeared to have no morals, love or compassion. They were extremely greedy and cruel in their pursuit of success.

An alarmed elder of a benevolent tribe called a conference of reasonable people in tribes throughout the region. They met to see what they might do to save these people from themselves. After much discussion, they decided to take the secret of personal success and happiness away from those who abused it and hide it from them. An elder asked, 'Where can we put it so they won't find it?' One person suggested it be buried deep in the earth, another on the top of a mountain. Some suggested it be thrown into the ocean. All concluded, however, that the secret of happiness and personal success could be found in any of these places. Finally an elder made this proposal: 'Let's hide the secret within the people themselves. People like this will never think to look for happiness and success there.'

To this day the warring tribe has continued to pursue success and happiness in many places, never guessing they possess it within.

The foolish man seeks
happiness in the distance;
the wise grows it
under his feet.

*. . . I have learned in whatever state
I am, to be content.*
Philippians 4:11 (NKJ)

A number of years ago, an old friend of John Wanamaker's came to Oak Hall to congratulate the famed department store owner on the store's sixtieth anniversary. He asked politely 'How do you keep?'

Wanamaker replied, 'Happily busy.'

Sixty years of uninterrupted work in one business is no small achievement. Wanamaker started his own business at the age of twenty-three and developed it into an establishment that became known worldwide. At eighty-three, he was still its head, and he was still making ambitious plans for the future.

His old friend asked him a second question, one that required Wanamaker to reflect on just how he had succeeded when so many others in his field had come and gone through the years. Wanamaker replied again: 'It is all the two words with which I answered your first question. Many people are busy because they have to be; I'm busy because I want to be. So I am happily busy.'

Rather than work to earn money so you can have the life you want . . . work at something you love and at which you are skilled, so that your work becomes a reflection of your very life. Success and money will follow and you will be satisfied and fulfilled.

Self-esteem isn't a
lesson you teach; it's a
quality you nurture.

*. . . but bring them up in the nurture
and admonition of the Lord.*
Ephesians 6:4 (KJV)

Marvin Allen tells of meeting Hugh Downs while Downs was taping a special on the men's movement. He writes:

'When I asked Hugh about his dad, his face lit up. He said that he remembered sitting in his dad's lap as a little boy talking with him for long periods of time. His dad would listen to him and nod thoughtfully making him feel both wise and worthy of his attention. He talked about the many times his father had taken him to the symphony and explained the names and sounds of the various instruments. He told me of visits to museums and how his dad had discussed art history with him in a way that made it seem fascinating, even to a little boy. As we got to Hugh's cabin, he said that his father had not only shared a great deal of information with him, he had communicated an overall enthusiasm for life.

'I could see how the joy of the father lived on in the son. Hugh's openness to new ideas, his compassion, and his wide-ranging interests are a testimony to how rich life can be for those fortunate men whose fathers were skilled in the art of dispensing usable love.'

When we do what we can, God will do what we can't.

For with God nothing shall be impossible.
Luke 1:37 (KJV)

A young man was running a race and he found himself falling further and further behind his competitors. His friends cheered him on from the sidelines, but seemingly to no avail. Then suddenly his lips began to move with great regularity, his legs picked up speed, and to the amazement and cheers of the entire crowd watching the race, he passed his competitors one by one . . . and won the race!

After he had been given a blue ribbon and received the congratulations of his coach and teammates, he turned to his friends. One of them asked, 'We could see your lips moving but we couldn't hear what you were saying. What were you mumbling out there?'

The young man replied, 'Oh, I was talking to God. I told Him, "Lord, You pick 'em up and I'll put 'em down . . . You pick 'em up and I'll put 'em down!" '

When we do the things we know to do, live our lives the way we know God's Word commands us, and we are believing to the best of our ability that the Lord will help us, we are then in a position to *know with certainty* what the Apostle Paul knew: 'I can do all things through Christ which strengtheneth me' (Philippians 4:13).

Seek God first and the things you want will seek you.

But seek first his kingdom and his righteousness, and all these things will be given to you as well.
Matthew 6:33 (NIV)

Dr George W. Truett once was entertained in the home of a wealthy oilman in Texas. After dinner, the man took Truett up to the roof of his home. Pointing to a field of oil derricks, he said, 'Dr Truett, that's all mine. I came to this country twenty-five years ago penniless, and now I own everything as far as you can see in that direction.'

He then turned in the opposite direction and, pointing towards waving fields of grain, he again said, 'It's all mine. I own everything as far as you can see in that direction.'

He next turned towards the east, pointing to a large herd of cattle . . . and then to the west, pointing to a great virgin forest that extended to the horizon . . . and each time he waved his hands and said, 'It's all mine. For twenty-five years I have worked hard and saved, and today I own everything you can see in any direction from my house.'

The man paused at that point, expecting words of admiration and praise from Truett. Instead, Dr Truett laid his hand lovingly on his shoulder, pointed upwards, and asked, 'And my friend, how much do you own in *that* direction?'

The strength of a man
consists in finding out
the way God is going,
and going that way.

*. . . I am the light of the world: he
that followeth me shall not walk in
darkness, but shall have the light of life.*
John 8:12 (KJV)

John Woolman, a 23-year-old clerk in a textiles shop, was busy adding up the day's receipts when his employer approached him with another man at his side and said, 'John, I've sold Nancy to this gentleman. Draw up a bill of sale for her.' As Woolman prepared to do so, something seemed to paralyse his arm. He could not write a word. He declared to his employer, a fellow Quaker, 'I believe slave-keeping to be a practice inconsistent with the Christian religion.'

The incident deeply troubled Woolman and shortly thereafter he wrote a pamphlet, *Some Considerations on the Keeping of Negroes,* which was printed by Benjamin Franklin in 1754. Although he became a tailor and orchard keeper, Woolman spent part of every year travelling to preach against slavery. He petitioned the Rhode Island legislature to abolish the slave trade. On a personal level, he stopped eating sugar and wearing indigo-dyed clothes, produced as the result of slave labour.

Eventually Woolman travelled to England in his crusade and his campaign of writing and speaking helped inspire William Wilberforce who after a prolonged battle in Parliament succeded in outlawing the slave trade in 1807 and abolishing slavery in all British colonies by 1833. One man – finding out the way – can change history.

I owe almost everything to my father.

*Honour your father and your mother, as
the LORD your God has commanded you.*

Deuteronomy 5:16 (NIV)

A proud father looked at the blue ribbon on the paper before him and began to read what his daughter had written: 'We [all] called him "Daddy" when we were young. He was able to make even folding clothes on Saturday fun with tickle fights amidst freshly washed garments strewn all over the living-room floor. He would roll and pretend at vulnerability on the carpet and grab each tiny groping hand that attempted to tweak his ribs. We seldom won, of course. Daddy could mercilessly tickle . . .

'There were serious times as well. He could spank the tears out of any of us, not because the physical pain was so incredible, but because it hurt us to think that we had brought him pain by having earned that spanking.

'High moral values, spiritual priorities, academic excellence – all these have been held out to us as important: My dad has instilled in us kids a sense of trust. He's been available, especially in emergencies. He has done what he thinks best for us, even when we might not agree . . . My dad has a corner on the upper echelons of fatherhood.'

What a tribute! One every father might desire . . . and *can* earn.

The more a child
becomes aware of
a father's willingness
to listen, the more
a father will
begin to hear.

He who has ears to hear, let him hear!
Matthew 11:15 (NKJ)

Best-selling author Leo Buscaglia's father was determined that each of his children would receive an education. He writes, 'Papa believed that the greatest sin was to go to bed at night as ignorant as when we awakened.' He insisted that each child learn at least one new thing each day. Dinnertime was the forum for sharing new facts and insights. Buscaglia says, 'The news we recounted, no matter how insignificant, was never taken lightly. Mama and Papa listened carefully and were ready with some comment, often profound and analytical, always to the point.' At the end of the meal, after Papa had lighted his cigar and taken stock of his family, came the question asked solemnly of each child, 'Tell me what you learned today.' Before the meal was over, the entire family had been enlightened by at least half a dozen facts.

Buscaglia notes, 'In retrospect, I realize what a dynamic educational technique Papa was offering us. Without being aware of it, our family was growing together, sharing experiences and participating in one another's education. And by looking at us, listening to us, respecting our input, affirming our value, giving us a sense of dignity, Papa was unquestionably our most influential teacher.'

Until you make peace
with who you are,
you'll never be
content with
what you have.

*But godliness with contentment
is great gain.*
1 Timothy 6:6 (KJV)

Christy Brown was born in Ireland in 1932 and raised in a Dublin slum. Born with a severe form of cerebral palsy, he could not walk, talk, eat or drink without help. He never went to school.

One day one of his siblings was on the floor, drawing letters on a piece of paper with crayons. Christy suddenly moved his left foot, managed to pick up and hold the crayon with his toes, and tried to copy the letters. From that day until his death in 1981, just using his left foot, typing with his little toe, he was able to write his autobiography, *My Left Foot*, which became a major motion picture. He also wrote two works of fiction. It took him fifteen years to type one of them, *Down All the Days*, but his effort resulted in his being hailed 'a man of genius' by the *New York Times*.

Christy Brown never moved from the slums. He fell in love and married. He was a man who first learned to accept his limitations . . . and then to rise above them!

Accept who you are and what you have today. And then *use what you have*. You'll likely find it's enough to bring you to a place of fulfilment in life.

A gentleman
is a gentle man.

As the Lord's servant, you must not
quarrel. You must be kind towards all, a
good and patient teacher, gentle . . .
2 Timothy 2:24 (GNB)

The last passenger to come aboard the flight was a man carried on a stretcher. Obviously paralysed from his shoulders down, he was strapped tightly into his seat. Once airborne, the hostesses began to serve the meal. A man noticed that a tray had been set before the paralysed man, but that it remained untouched. Seeing that the hostesses were all busy serving other passengers, he slipped into a seat next to the man and asked if he might help. The paralysed man responded, 'Thank you. I would be so grateful.'

As the man cut the first few bites and placed them in the paralysed man's mouth, he felt awkward, but at the same time, much needed. Before long, the two were co-ordinating bites well and they began to talk. The paralysed man told of his unfortunate accident, his lonesomeness, his joys, his struggles, his faith. They exchanged names. In a strange way their spirits blended. The helpful man later concluded, 'We experienced sacrament' – a truly sacred moment.

How many people are there who have had the Good News about Jesus Christ set before them, yet they are crippled by spiritual and psychological paralysis . . . and there's no one to feed them? It takes a gentle man to feed a person who cannot feed himself.

(The called man) sees himself as a steward . . . He's obedient rather than ambitious, committed rather than competitive. For him, nothing is more important than pleasing the One who called him.

. . . because we obey his commands and do what pleases him.
1 John 3:22 (NIV)

Stewardship is not something a person decides to do after he or she has made a lot of money. Being a steward is part of being a Christian. Stewardship is the requirement that a person take care of his financial affairs as if he was managing the earthly finances of the Lord Himself.

Walt Meloon once had this to say about the relationship between business and God:

'A businessman has no business being in business just to make money. Every businessman automatically is in danger of making money his god. Whenever he makes a decision in favour of his business as opposed to the Lord Jesus Christ, he has made money his god, for the moment, at least. He is favouring mammon, and his priorities are mixed.

'Advice not to mix Christianity and business is heresy of the worst kind. A man's business, whatever it might be, ought to be an integrated and integral part of his Christianity. It either complements or opposes his spiritual stance.'

No matter how hard you try, you cannot separate what you have from who you are, and who you are is defined ultimately by who you are to Christ Jesus.

If I take care of my
character, my reputation
will take care of itself.

Righteousness guards
the man of integrity.
Proverbs 13:6 (NIV)

The story is told of a king who owned a valuable diamond, a rare and almost flawless gem. One day the diamond fell and a deep scratch marred its face. The king summoned the best diamond experts in the land to correct the blemish, but they all agreed they could not remove the scratch without cutting away a good part of the surface, thus reducing the weight and value of the diamond.

Finally one expert appeared and assured him that he could fix the diamond without reducing its value. His self-confidence was convincing and the king gave the diamond to the man. In a few days, the artisan returned the diamond to the king, who was amazed to find that the ugly scratch was gone, and in its place was etched a beautiful rose. The former scratch had become the stem of an exquisite flower!

An error we make in life may temporarily mar our reputation. But if we stick to what we know is right and continue to attempt to conform our will to that of God, we can trust Him to turn the 'scratches' on our souls into part of His signature – a signature of inner character that truly *becomes* our eternal reputation.

Remember, when your child has a tantrum, don't have one of your own.

Refrain from anger and turn from wrath;
do not fret – it leads only to evil.
Psalm 37:8 (NIV)

A little boy had moved with his parents to a house overlooking a deep ravine. One day his mother reprimanded him for disobeying her and he became very angry, stormed out of the house, and ran to the edge of the ravine. There, to give vent to his feelings, he shouted as loud as he could, 'I hate you! I hate you!' Almost immediately, a voice came rumbling back at him in an angry, hollow voice, 'I hate you! I hate you!' Startled at first, and then terrified, the little boy raced back into the house. Once in the safety of his mother's arms, he told her there was a wicked man in the ravine who hated him and wanted to do him harm.

The wise mother took her son by the hand and led him back to the ravine. In a tender and cheerful voice she called, 'I love you! I love you!' A kind, happy voice echoed back the same sweet words, much to the boy's comfort and delight.

The tantrums of our children can easily disturb us, frustrate us and even anger us. But just as your child has the ability to impact your mood . . . so you have the ability to impact his! By responding with kindness and good cheer, you can usually turn around a child's tantrum and maintain your own bright outlook on life at the same time.

Children are not so
different from kites . . .
Children were created
to fly but they need wind
– the undergirding and
strength that comes from
unconditional love,
encouragement
and prayer.

*. . . as a father deals with his own
children, encouraging, comforting and
urging you to live lives worthy of God . . .*
1 Thessalonians 2:11,12 (NIV)

When he was just a boy, John's father made a journey with his family across the American continent. It took the family a full year to make their way from coast to coast. As each sunset and sunrise glorified the skies, the Scotsman would take his children out to show them the skies and speak to them about how the cloud formations were surely 'the robes of God'.

Who can fathom the full impact this trip had on young John? Or how deeply rooted became his reverence for nature on this year-long journey? What we do know is that John Muir became one of America's greatest naturalists. His love for nature led him to the mountains, the glacial meadows and eventually to the icebound bays of Alaska. The lovely Muir Woods in northern California are named in his honour.

What are you 'showing' your children today? What 'wind' are you putting under their wings? What examples . . . what encouragements . . . what insights are you giving to your child?

As the Helen Reddy song declared so poignantly more than two decades ago: 'You are the wind beneath my wings' – so a parent's influence is for each child.

When these parenting
years have passed
something precious will
have flickered
and gone out of
my life. Thus, I am
resolved to enjoy every
day that remains in
this fathering era.

Redeeming the time . . .
Ephesians 5:16 (KJV)

Howard was a man in tune with the times. So, when his four-year-old daughter, Melinda, acquired a fixation for *The Three Little Pigs* and demanded that her father read it to her night after night, Howard took action. He bought a child's easy-to-use tape recorder and read the story onto tape for her.

The next time Melinda asked for the story to be read, he switched on the recorder. She was fascinated at the novelty of her father's voice reading her favourite book from a 'machine'. The following night when she asked for 'Free Li'l Pigs', Howard went a step further: he showed Melinda how to work the playback on the recorder for herself.

The following evening, when Melinda arrived and pushed the storybook at him, Howard said, 'Now, honey you know how to turn on the recorder.' She smiled and said sweetly but insistently 'Yes,' and then added, 'but I can't sit on its lap.'

Children need both a father's time and an expression of his affection, including hugs and being held close. A 'close' relationship is generally rooted in just that – holding a child close to one's heart always, and close to one's side until it's *the child's idea* to move to the other end of the sofa.

He that will have
his son respect him and
his orders must have
a great reverence
for his son.

*Fathers, do not exasperate your children;
instead, bring them up in the training
and instruction of the Lord.*
Ephesians 6:4 (NIV)

One winter day in Rockefeller Center in New York, a man watched the skaters whirling about on the ice. He found himself drawn to one pair: a teenage girl who was receiving instruction from a brilliant skater. She moved around the rink, making a large circle close to the edge; her instructor skated a smaller circle towards the centre of the rink, executing classical figures even as he kept his eye on her every move. It was easy to see that she was not sure of herself. Several times she nearly fell. But each time she began to become unsteady in a flash he was by her side, his hand on her elbow helping her maintain her balance.

He said to himself, 'What a perfect picture of the life to which the Lord Jesus has called us! God has given to many of us the gift of helping those who are younger . . . or who are in need!' How true this is for fathers especially. A father is called to keep his eye always upon his children, ready to help, but without show. The unsteady one will know he has been helped, and that the touch at the right moment kept him from falling. But the world will scarcely notice. He will know and the Lord will know, and that is sufficient.

10 COMMANDMENTS FOR EFFECTIVE FATHERS

No. 1
Spend time with your children.

Making the very most of the time –
buying up each opportunity . . .
Ephesians 5:16 (AMP)

A man once had a job that required extensive travel. After every long trip, his wife and four children would meet him at the door with loving hugs and kisses. After one such joyful homecoming, he was playing with his youngest child and he asked her, 'What do you want to be when you grow up?' The child responded without hesitation, 'A pilot.'

'Why a pilot?' the father asked, a bit surprised.

His daughter looked at him and replied, 'So I can spend more time with you.' Shortly thereafter, the father took a position that required far less travel!

Most people have a 'career lifespan' of forty to fifty years. Experts agree that what an average person earns in the last half of their career is nearly double that of the first half. Parents, by comparison, usually have only twenty to twenty-five years of 'active parenting'. Even so, many people place far greater emphasis on work during the first half of their career life than they do on family to the detriment of their children and with not much career advancement. Consider another approach! Place emphasis on your *family* during the first twenty years of your career, and then devote full energy to your work during the years when you are wiser, more skilled and able to earn the most!

10 COMMANDMENTS FOR
EFFECTIVE FATHERS

No. 2
Let your children know often that you love them just the way they are.

Accept one another, then, for the glory of God, as Christ has accepted you.

Romans 15:7 (GNB)

'The Hole in the Wall Gang Camp' was designed and built through the vision and efforts of actor Paul Newman and a group of dedicated volunteers. Opened in 1988, the camp is located on three hundred acres of forest in north-eastern Connecticut. It was designed to resemble an Old West logging town of the 1890s. The buildings, facilities and site make possible a wide range of activities: swimming in a heated outdoor pool, boating, canoeing, fishing, horseback riding, nature walks, woodworking, music, theatre, arts, crafts, sports, overnight camping. Children from seven to seventeen come to the camp during the summer's four, 10-day sessions.

Sounds like any other summer camp? Hardly. What makes this camp unique, apart from the fact that no camper is charged a fee, is that it accepts *only* children who have cancer, leukaemia and other serious blood diseases – children who, because of their disease, its treatment or its complications, cannot attend ordinary camps. The facilities are equipped to meet the medical and physical needs of these special children.

If the founders of a summer camp can accept and love children 'just the way they are', how much more should we love and accept our own children.

10 COMMANDMENTS FOR EFFECTIVE FATHERS

No. 3
Discipline your children when they need it.

*He who spares the rod hates
his son, but he who loves him
is diligent to discipline him.*
Proverbs 13:24 (RSV)

A grandfather once found his grandson jumping up and down in his playpen, crying at the top of his voice. When Joey saw his grandfather, he reached up his chubby hands and cried all the louder, 'Out, Gamba, out!'

The grandfather naturally reached down to lift Joey out of his predicament, but as he did, Joey's mother said, 'No, Joey you are being punished – so you must stay in your playpen.'

The grandfather felt at a loss as to what to do. On the one hand, he knew he must comply with the mother's efforts to discipline her son. On the other hand, Joey's tears and uplifted hands tugged at his heart. Love found a way! If Gamba couldn't take his grandson out of the playpen, he could climb in and join him there!

Discipline, in its finest form, is 'directing a child towards a better way'. Discipline goes beyond punishment for a deed to the instilling in a child a desire never to repeat the offending deed, and instead, make a better choice of behaviours. The desire to do right is born of love – the love of the parent for the child and, more importantly, the love of the parent shown to the child.

10 COMMANDMENTS FOR
EFFECTIVE FATHERS

No. 4
Pray with and for
your child regularly.

With this in mind, we constantly
pray for you.
2 Thessalonians 1:11 (NIV)

To hear my child at prayer,
What a thrill it is for me!
There's a sweetness in the moment
As he speaks on bended knee.
And yet my heart is smitten
At this touching sight I see,
Has his faith and trust in prayer
Depended much on me?
As I see him fold his tiny hands
And bow his head to pray,
I trust he'll always love the Lord
The way he does today.
Then I hear a voice within me
Speak in solemn words and true,
'How he lives a life of prayer
Depends a lot on you.'
And so I kneel next to the bed,
And lay my hand upon him
After he has voiced his prayer,
I add my own petition.
May my son recall one day
That his father daily raised
His voice to thank the Lord
And make sacrifice of praise!

10 COMMANDMENTS FOR
EFFECTIVE FATHERS

No. 5
Always be honest
with your children.

A good man is known by his truthfulness;
a false man by deceit and lies.

Proverbs 12:17 (TLB)

When baseball player, Dave Dravecky, first noticed the lump on his pitching arm, he had it checked out, but nothing seemed amiss. The lump continued to grow, however, and eventually Dravecky had it biopsied. The result came back: a form of cancer called fibrosarcoma. The treatment called for aggressive surgery to cut away a large part of the bone. Physicians held out little hope he would ever pitch again.

Dave and his wife Janice decided to tell their children, Tiffany and Jonathan, what was happening. As they tucked them into bed one night, they gently explained that Daddy was going to be in the hospital for a while, and that he probably wouldn't be able to play baseball anymore. They waited for the news to sink in, thinking it would devastate them. Tiffany however, responded by saying, 'You mean we won't have to move anymore? I can stay in my same school? We'll be here in Ohio near Grandma and Grandpa all the time?' Jonathan joined in, 'Dad, you mean you'll be able to play football with me every day?'

As much as anything else, their reaction helped Dave Dravecky cope with what lay ahead. In his words, they 'put it all into perspective'. Be honest with your children. They may help you see things in a new light!

10 COMMANDMENTS FOR
EFFECTIVE FATHERS

No. 6
Love your
children's mother.

*And you husbands, show the same kind
of love to your wives as Christ showed
to the church when he died for her.*

Ephesians 5:25 (TLB)

Helmut Thielicke writes in *How the World Began,* 'I once knew a very old married couple who radiated a tremendous happiness. The wife especially, who was almost unable to move because of old age and illness and in whose kind old face the joys and sufferings of many years had etched a hundred lines, was filled with such a gratitude for life that I was touched to the quick. Involuntarily I asked myself what could possibly be the source of this kindly person's radiance. In every other respect they were common people, and their room indicated only the most modest comfort. But suddenly I knew where it all came from, for I saw those two speaking to each other, and their eyes hanging upon each other. All at once it became clear to me that this woman was dearly loved.

'It was not because she was a cheerful and pleasant person that she was loved by her husband all those years. It was the other way around. Because she was so loved she became the person I saw before me.'

You cannot expect your children to show greater respect for their mother – or their own spouses someday – than you show to her.

10 COMMANDMENTS FOR
EFFECTIVE FATHERS

No. 7
Take time to listen
to your children.

Let the wise listen and add
to their learning.
Proverbs 1:5 (NIV)

Jed Harris, the producer of *Our Town* and numerous other plays, became convinced he was losing his hearing. He went to one physician who couldn't find anything wrong. He referred him to a specialist.

The specialist gave Harris a thorough checkup and nothing showed up to indicate a physical problem with Harris' hearing. The doctor finally pulled out a gold watch and asked, 'Can you hear this ticking?'

Harris said, 'Of course.'

The specialist walked to the door of the examining room and held up the watch again. 'Now can you hear it?' he asked.

Harris concentrated and said, 'Yes, I can hear it clearly.'

Finally the doctor walked out of the door into the next room and called, 'Can you hear it now?'

Harris said, 'Yes.'

The specialist came back into the examining room and announced, 'Mr Harris, there is nothing wrong with your hearing. You just don't listen.'

Really *listen* to your children today. You may be amazed at what you learn from them.

No. 8
Encourage your children often.

*Therefore encourage one another and
build each other up . . .*
1 Thessalonians 5:11 (NIV)

Author Phyllis Theroux writes about her father, 'If there was any one thing that my father did for me when I was growing up it was to give me the promise that ahead of me was dry land – a bright, marshless territory, without chuckholes or traps, where one day I would walk easily and as befitting my talents . . .

'Thus it was, when he came upon me one afternoon sobbing out my unsuccesses into a wet pillow, that he sat down on the bed and . . . assured me that my grief was only a temporary setback. Oh, very temporary! Why, he couldn't think of any other little girl who was so talented, so predestined to succeed in every department as I was. "And don't forget," he added with a smile, "that we can trace our ancestry right back to Pepin the Stupid!"

'By the time he had finished talking I really did understand that someday I would live among rational beings, and walk with kind, unvindictive people who, by virtue of their maturity and mine, would take no pleasure in cruelty and would welcome my presence among them . . . There are some people who carry the flint that lights other people's torches. They get them all excited about . . . the "can-do" potential of one's own being. That was my father's gift to me.'

10 COMMANDMENTS FOR
EFFECTIVE FATHERS

No. 9
Celebrate your children's achievements.

Rejoice with them that do rejoice.
Romans 12:15 (KJV)

Political commentator, George F Will, has written lovingly about his son: 'Jon Frederick Will, the oldest of my four children, recently turned 21, and on his birthday as he does on every workday he commuted by subway to his job delivering mail and being useful in other ways at the National Institutes of Health. That my son is striding into a productive manhood with a spring in his step and Baltimore Orioles on his mind could not have been confidently predicted when he was born . . . Jon has Down's syndrome. At the instant he was conceived, he lost one of life's lotteries, but he also was lucky: his physical abnormalities do not impede his vitality, and his mental retardation does not interfere with life's essential joys – receiving love, returning it and reading baseball box scores.

'So one must mind one's language when speaking of people like Jon. He does not "suffer from" Down's syndrome. It is an affliction, but he is happy . . . Happiness, in fact, is a talent, for which Jon has a superior aptitude . . . One aspect of Jon's abnormality . . . is that he is gentleness straight through. Jon is an adornment in a world increasingly stained by anger acted out. He was born on his father's birthday, a gift that keeps on giving.'

10 COMMANDMENTS FOR
EFFECTIVE FATHERS

No. 10
Be flexible with
your children.

*Be patient with each other, making
allowance for each other's faults
because of your love.*
Ephesians 4:2b (TLB)

Stonecutters use an interesting process to engrave granite. They first paint over a slab of polished granite with a thin coating of rubber. The design for the engraving is pencilled onto the rubber and then the rubber is cut away leaving the stone exposed where the design is to appear. Using compressed air, the stonecutter then blows sand against the granite slab. Where the stone is exposed, the sand cuts into the granite and creates the etching. The areas covered with rubber remain unaffected.

Sand can be blown upon the rubber for an hour without making an imprint, even though sand blown against granite for that long would probably bore a hole completely through the hardest slab. Why? The stone resists stubbornly and is worn away but the rubber is resilient and absorbs the shock without damage.

How resilient and flexible are you with your child? Do you offer resistance to their high-energy, erratic behaviour, so that they wear you out? Or do you accept your child's unpredictability and energy as a part of life, going with the flow of their moods and interests in a way that leaves you personally unscathed? When in the presence of your child, think rubber instead of granite. You'll last longer!

'A merry heart doeth good like a medicine . . .'

Proverbs 17:22

There is a right time for everything:
. . . A time to laugh . . .

Ecclesiastes 3:1,4 (TLB)

A boy devoted an entire rainy afternoon to a drawing. On a large piece of paper, he drew and drew, periodically stepping back to take stock of his masterpiece. From his father's vantage point, the boy seemed to be using every crayon in his 64-crayon pack. Curious and a little surprised at the patience and persistence of his son, the father finally went over to the table where he was working and looked over his shoulder. The scribbles and colour patches didn't seem to make much sense to him, so he asked, as innocently as possible, 'What's that you are drawing, son?'

The boy answered, 'God.' With concern that his child might be making a theological error, the father said, 'Oh, son, nobody knows what God looks like.'

Undaunted and hardly pausing, his son replied with assurance, 'They will when I'm finished.'

Many jokes and humorous stories are about children or relay the quips of children as they explore life. Perhaps that is to be expected. Children tend to have a fresher look at life, and are eager to giggle at what they perceive to be life's foibles. Perhaps that's why the Lord admonished each of us to become like little children – so we could enjoy life, each other and the Father more!

There are three ways
to get something done:
do it yourself,
hire someone,
or forbid your kids
to do it.

A merry heart does good, like medicine.
Proverbs 17:22 (NKJ)

Teresa Bloomingdale offers these humorous suggestions for improving family communication:

1. If you have tiny children who won't give you their attention, simply place a long-distance telephone call to somebody important, preferably their grandmother. Your toddlers will immediately climb up on your lap and become all ears.

2. Lure your wife into the bedroom and lock the door. The entire family will immediately converge in the hallway insisting they must talk to you.

3. Get a job in an office that discourages personal phone calls. Your kids will then call you every hour on the hour.

4. Send them away to college or let them move into an apartment. They can then be counted on . . . for long chats, during which they will expound at length on what wonderful parents you were, and what happened, because you certainly are spoiling their younger siblings rotten.

A father is someone
who carries pictures
where his money
used to be.

For everything there is a season . . .
a time to laugh.
Ecclesiastes 3:1,4 (RSV)

Two young 'toughs' stood at a certain corner in Brooklyn, hiding themselves round the edge of a building, waiting for a certain man. They had watched this man pass the corner at precisely 6:30 each evening, laden with grocery bags and a lunch box. They had also spied the outline of a fat wallet in his hip pocket under his short jacket. It seemed obvious to them that he brought his pay home each day in cash – cash they eagerly anticipated would be theirs with only a few clever moves and the element of surprise on their side.

Promptly at 6:30 the man appeared, striding with a purpose born of having somewhere meaningful to go. The boys tensed and then sprang from their hiding place. The attack was over in an instant. Before he really knew what had hit him, the man was lying on the ground, his head swimming, groceries scattered around him. The thugs raced two streets away down an alley. 'Whew! Man!' they laughed. 'Let's see how much we got!' Four hands scrambled to open the bulging wallet. Their eyes grew wide as they surveyed the contents – two dollars and two long foldouts of picture after picture of the man's six children.

To Men Over 40:
Don't worry about losing
hair – think of it
as gaining face.

*A cheerful heart does good
like medicine . . .*
Proverbs 17:22 (TLB)

Baseball great, Joe Garagiola, also a former broad-caster and host of the *Today* show, wrote about his own baldness:

'Actually, being bald isn't so bad. It has some definite advantages. In any room you're the first to know the location of the air-conditioning ducts. Outdoors, you're the first to know if it's starting to rain . . .

'When you're bald, forgetting a comb or a hair dryer doesn't cause any panic.

'The biggest advantage is that you're windproof. A man who wears a toupee actually has to walk leaning into a strong wind. I'm sure I'll get some arguments from the hairpiece makers, but every man I've ever been around who wears a piece needs to know which way the flags are blowing. He can't pass a mirror or a window without checking it, to see not only if it's on straight, but if it's still on at all. A man with styled hair or a transplant really has problems with the wind. I've seen men literally walk on an angle, looking deformed, to battle the wind. The bald head has the edge. What can the wind do to us? We couldn't get our hair messed up in a hurricane.'

Many a father wishes
he was strong enough
to tear a telephone
book in two –
especially if he has
a teenage daughter.

There is a time for everything . . .
a time to laugh . . .
Ecclesiastes 3:1,4 (NIV)

Long before the days of 'call waiting', a certain teenage daughter seemed to be on the phone constantly. No sooner would one caller hang up than the phone would ring again. One day her father answered six consecutive calls for her, and decided upon answering the seventh call, to try a little humour. He answered, 'Congratulations! You have reached my daughter's phone. Unfortunately you are only the seventh caller and she is currently taking every tenth call.' The man heard no teenage giggles, no stammering words, only silence. Concerned that his sense of humour had not been appreciated, he tried a tentative 'Hello?'

A very businesslike voice then said, 'This is the library. We have the book you requested we put on hold. Perhaps you can dash over here during the tenth call and pick it up.'

Speaking of call waiting . . . A father was once seen making a call using his cellular phone. His wife asked, 'Why are you using the mobile phone in the bedroom?' He replied, 'Our daughter is on the phone and I need to talk to her. She always interrupts her calls to answer a call-waiting signal, so I figure this is the best way to get a word in edgewise!'

A father is a person
who is forced to
endure childbirth
without an
anaesthetic.

Being cheerful keeps you healthy.
Proverbs 17:22 (GNB)

A young father-to-be was found pacing back and forth in a hospital waiting room, wringing his hands, while his wife was in labour. Occasionally he would peer through the windows of the swinging doors, and then quickly glance away.

'You could have been in there helping her,' another father suggested. 'It might have been less stressful.'

'Oh, no!' the young man exclaimed. 'I probably would have fainted dead away and that wouldn't have been helpful at all.'

Hours passed. The young man was soon tied up in knots of fear and anxiety, beads of perspiration dropping from his brow. He truly appeared to be suffering. Finally at four o'clock in the morning a nurse came through the door and announced cheerfully, 'You have a beautiful, healthy little girl.'

The young man dropped his hands at his sides, slumped down into a chair and sighed, 'Oh, thank God it's a girl. She'll never have to go through the awful agony I've had tonight.'

Before I got married,
I had six theories
about bringing up
children: now I
have six children
and no theories.

For everything there is a season . . .
a time to laugh . . .
Ecclesiastes 3:1,4 (RSV)

In sharing his own 'theory' about raising a child, social commentator, Andy Rooney, has written: 'I know what I think every child should have [to grow] up to become a responsible, honest, producing member of our society instead of a sad welfare case or a prison inmate. He or she should have:

- A home with one mother and one father
- A family that eats dinner together
- A room of his or her own, even if it's tiny
- A good night kiss
- A warm bed with a blanket or quilt that has its own character, under which the kid can hide
- A sweet, motherly kindergarten teacher
- A cake with candles to blow out with a wish on every birthday
- A place to swim . . . and sleigh-ride.
- A friend to whom he or she can tell secrets
- Some minor illnesses to let the child know that life isn't always a bowl of cherries
- A rich uncle or a doting aunt
- Talent. Every child should be encouraged to be good at something, no matter how minor a talent it is
- Discipline
- Someone to read aloud to him or her

Fatherhood is pretending the present you love most is soap-on-a-rope.

A cheerful heart is good medicine . . .
Proverbs 17:22 (NIV)

A minister once found his young son tiptoeing into his study while he was working on a sermon. He had left explicit instructions that he was not to be disturbed. 'What do you want, Michael?' he asked sternly. 'Nothing,' the boy answered, 'I just wanted to be with you.' As you might imagine, the response melted the father's heart. Rather than a reprimand, his son received a hug.

Such a father surely was justified in feeling disturbed at being interrupted. But . . . he was wise enough to allow his love for his child to overshadow and overrule his first response.

In his book *Hide or Seek*, Dr James Dobson lists what he believes to be the five most common barriers that cause children to doubt their worth or that they are pleasing to their parents – even when they are deeply loved. The first barrier is that of 'parental insensitivity'. Sensitivity is tuning into the thoughts and feelings of a child, listening to the clues he gives, and reacting appropriately. The sensitive heart rubs its fingers along the edges of a child's soul, feeling for the deep cracks, the snags, taking the time to hear, to care, to give, to share.

Remember, the next time your child gives you a gift you have no use for, turn on your sensitivity scanner so as not to damage your child's heart.

Old boys have their
playthings just like the
young ones; the difference
is only in the price.

There is a right time for everything . . .
a time to laugh . . .
Ecclesiastes 3:1,4 (TLB)

A man once moved from Massachusetts to Florida and, a few days after unpacking, decided to see if the area's reputation for good fishing was deserved. He assembled the tackle that he had used successfully for freshwater fishing up north and then settled in at a popular spot along the Intracoastal Waterway. He attached his favourite bait to his line and cast out. Within minutes, he caught a magnificent eight-pound fish.

The local fishermen gazed in admiration as the newcomer brought the big catch ashore. He offered it to one of the spectators to examine. The old pro balanced it in his hands and asked, 'Now, what kind of bait did you use to land this beauty?' The man replied, 'I used my favourite silver spinner.'

'Oh, no,' the old-timer responded. 'You can't catch anything on that. You've got to use live shrimp in these waters.'

Inexpensive lines sometimes catch just as big a fish as expensive rods. Inexpensive cameras sometimes take just as good a photograph as expensive cameras. An inexpensive putter can sink a ball just as well as an expensive one – but don't try to convince the owner of more expensive equipment!

A major problem
these days is how
to save money for
your children's college
education when you're
still paying for yours.

A cheerful heart does good
like medicine . . .
Proverbs 17:22 (TLB)

Bill Cosby writes in *Fatherhood*, 'A father like me, with five children, faces the terrifying prospect of sending five to college. When my oldest one went, the bill for her first year had already reached thirteen thousand dollars. I looked hard at this bill and then said to her, "Thirteen thousand dollars. Will you be the only student?" . . .

'I multiplied thirteen thousand times four, added another thirty thousand for incidentals during these four years, and got the sum of eighty-two thousand dollars that I would be spending to see my daughter pick up a liberal arts degree, which would qualify her to come back home.

'One day last year, my eighteen-year-old daughter came in and told my wife and me that she had decided not to go to college because she was in love with a boy named Alan. At first, my wife and I went crazy . . . and then a light went on in one of the musty corners of my mind: her decision would be saving me a hundred thousand dollars.

' " . . . not going to college, which you have every right to tell us. Alan, you say? Well, he just happens to be the one I'm exceptionally fond of. I hope he's feeling well. Would you like me to send him to Palm Beach for a couple of weeks to get a little sun?" '

A boy becomes an adult
three years before his
parents think he does,
and about two years
after he thinks he does.

There is a time for everything . . .
a time to laugh . . .
Ecclesiastes 3:1,4 (NIV)

On his sixteenth birthday a son approached his father and asked, 'When I get my licence, Dad, can I drive the family car?'

The father replied, 'Son, driving the car takes maturity and first, I want you to prove to me you are responsible enough. One way you can prove your maturity to me is to bring up your grades, which I know you are capable of doing. Second, I want you to read your Bible every day. And finally I want you to get a haircut.'

The son began the task of fulfilling his father's requirements. The next time school reports were issued, he came to his father with a big smile and said, 'Look, Dad, all As and Bs. Now can I drive the car?'

'Great, son,' the father said. 'You're one-third of the way there. Have you been reading the Bible daily?'

'Yes,' the boy replied.

'Fine. You're two-thirds there. Now, when are you going to get that hair cut?'

The son thought for a moment and said, 'I don't see why I should get my hair cut to drive the car. Jesus had long hair, didn't He?' The father replied, 'That's right, and Jesus walked everywhere He went.'

Before marriage, a
man will lie awake all
night thinking about
something you said;
after marriage,
he'll fall asleep before
you finish saying it.

A merry heart does good,
like medicine.
Proverbs 17:22 (NKJ)

A humorist once identified the following as a husband's reactions to his wife's colds during seven years of their marriage:

FIRST YEAR: 'Sugar dumpling, I'm really worried about you. You've got a bad sniffle and there's no telling about these things. I'm driving you to the hospital for a general checkup.'

SECOND YEAR: 'Listen, darling, I don't like the sound of that cough and I've called Dr Miller to come over. Now you go to bed.'

THIRD YEAR: 'Maybe you'd better lie down, honey. Nothing like a little rest when you feel lousy. I'll bring you something. Have we got any cans of soup?'

FOURTH YEAR: 'Now look, dear, be sensible. After you've fed the kids and done the dishes, you'd better lie down.'

FIFTH YEAR: 'Why don't you take a couple of aspirin?'

SIXTH YEAR: 'I wish you'd just gargle or something instead of sitting around barking like a seal all evening.'

SEVENTH YEAR: 'For Pete's sake, stop sneezing. Are you trying to give me pneumonia?'

Is it not strange that
he who has no
children brings
them up so well?

To every thing there is a season . . .
a time to laugh . . .
Ecclesiastes 3:1,4 (KJV)

Screenwriter William Goldman once noted that, in spite of all the experience that Hollywood people have in making movies, 'Nobody knows anything.' The same may be true about raising children.

One thing Bill Cosby found when he conducted his own Cosby Poll of parents, was that most parents didn't even know why they had had their children! He writes, 'I have gotten answers that almost made sense:

'Because I wanted someone to carry on the family name.

'Because a child will be an enduring reflection of ourselves.

'Because I wanted someone to look after me in my old age.

'Because we wanted to hear sounds around the house.'

He concludes, however, that he did finally find one shining exception in his poll: 'One day I found a woman who was the mother of six children; and with simple eloquence, she explained to me why she'd had them. "Because," she said, "I kept falling asleep." '

Once here . . . always yours. That's the guarantee that comes with every baby born!

The young man
knows the rules,
but the old
man knows
the exceptions.

A merry heart does good, like medicine . .

.

Proverbs 17:22 (NKJ)

One of New York City's most popular mayors was Fiorello LaGuardia. Nearly every older New Yorker has a favourite memory of him. Some recall the day he read the funny papers over the radio, with all the appropriate inflections, after a strike kept the Sunday newspapers off the stands. Others remember his outbursts against the 'bums' who exploited the poor.

One time the mayor chose to preside in a night court. An old woman was brought before him on the bitterly cold night. The charge was stealing a loaf of bread. She explained as her reason for the theft that her family was starving. LaGuardia replied, 'I've got to punish you. The law makes no exception. I must fine you ten dollars.' At that, he reached into his own pocket and pulled out a ten-dollar bill. 'Well,' he said, 'here's the ten dollars to pay your fine, which I now remit.' He then tossed the ten-dollar bill into his own hat and declared, 'I'm going to fine everybody in this courtroom fifty cents for living in a town where a person has to steal bread in order to eat. Mr Bailiff, collect the fines and give them to this defendant.'

After the hat was passed, the incredulous old woman left the courtroom with a new light in her eyes and $47.50 in her pocket to buy groceries!

Father: A man who
can't get on the phone,
into the bathroom, or
out of the house.

There is a right time for everything . . .
a time to laugh . . .
Ecclesiastes 3:1,4 (TLB)

A father once found this note pinned to the bulletin board by the family phone:

Daddy – I am going to wash my hair. If Tom calls, tell him to call at eight. If Herb calls and Tom doesn't, tell Herb to call at eight, but if they both call, tell Herb to call at 8:15 or 8:30. If Timmy calls, and Tom and Herb don't, tell Timmy to call at eight, but if they both call (Tom & Herb) or one calls, tell Timmy to call at 8:30 or 8:40. Tina.

Speaking of phones . . .

The Illinois Bell Telephone Company has reported that the volume of long-distance calls being made on Father's Day is growing! In fact, the numbers are growing faster than the number of calls being made on Mother's Day.

In issuing the report, the company apologized for the delay in compiling the statistics, but explained that the 'extra billing' of calls was the reason for the slow tabulation. It seems that most of the calls to fathers on Father's Day were made . . . 'collect'.

In a perfect world . . .
teenagers would
much rather work
on the lawn than
talk on the telephone.

Being cheerful keeps you healthy.
Proverbs 17:22 (GNB)

In *Up a Family Tree,* Teresa Bloomingdale writes: 'As I was soaking in the tub, the phone in our bedroom rang and rang and rang. I knew my husband was in the basement, so I yelled at the kids: "Why doesn't somebody answer that?" They yelled back: "You told us we couldn't talk on your phone!"

'Later I carefully explained to them that they could answer the main line; they just couldn't call out on it.

'The next day I again tried to call out on the kitchen main line, and again the extension was busy. I checked the front hall; nobody talking on that phone; it was buried under books and boots.

'I went upstairs and found Peggy perched on my bed, cheerfully chatting away on my telephone. "I thought I told you not to use that telephone," I scolded her. "But you said to answer it if it rang; it rang, and when I answered it, it was for me," she said. "Well tell your friends to call you on the teen line," I told her. "Oh this isn't my friend," said Peg. "This is Annie. She's downstairs and wanted to ask me something, so she called me from downstairs. Isn't this neat?" '

When I was a boy of fourteen my father was so ignorant I could hardly stand to have the old man around. But when I got to be twenty-one I was astonished at how much the old man had learned in seven years.

There is a right time for everything . . .
a time to laugh . . .
Ecclesiastes 3:1,4 (TLB)

A young woman confided to her minister one day 'I am afraid I sin each morning.' The minister replied, 'What makes you think so?' She answered, 'Because every morning when I gaze into the mirror, I think how beautiful I am.' The minister took a second look at the young woman before him and announced, 'Never fear. That isn't a sin; it's only a mistake.'

Egotism comes in many forms, but one positive thing about this brand of pride is that it often dissipates with age. Consider this progression of comments . . .

A child of five who has just completed a puzzle, 'Daddy, daddy I can do just about everything.'

A twenty-one year old: 'Just ask me anything!'

A forty-year-old: 'If it's in my line, I can tell you because I know my business like an open book.'

A man of fifty: 'The field of human knowledge is so vast that even a specialist can hardly know all of it.'

A man of seventy: 'I've lived a good many years and I've come to realize that what I know is little and what I don't know is vast.'

A man of ninety: 'I really don't know much, and I can't recall even more.'

A father is a thing
that grows when it
feels good . . . and
laughs very loud
when its scared
half to death.

A merry heart doeth good
like a medicine.
Proverbs 17:22 (KJV)

In *I Want to Grow Hair, I Want to Grow Up, I Want to Go to Boise*, Erma Bombeck compares the reality of fathers' responses to that of the TV image of fathers. She writes:

'If a demolition ball like cancer hits the family while they're gone, it's business as usual. *I'm a salesman and I'd be driving down the highway and I'd pull over and bawl for forty-five minutes . . .*

'Fathers have a reputation for going through life like they have bodies shot full of novocaine. They're cool. They have a certain dignity and distance . . .

My Dad won a trip to Orlando, Florida, for me when he entered a Jell-O Gelatin Jump. For this he had to jump into four hundred gallons of strawberry Jell-O. I never thought my Dad would do this.

'Fathers are also endowed with a strength and detachment that permits them . . . not to fall apart. *When Ken decided to share responsibilities with his wife he accompanied his daughter, Mary Beth, to her spinal tap. When Mary Beth groaned, Ken turned white as a sheet and fainted dead away.*'

Bombeck concludes: 'So much for Father Teresa and so much for the three popular myths surrounding fathers. The truth is men are just as vulnerable.'

It now costs more
to amuse a child
than it once did to
educate his father.

For everything there is a season . . .
a time to laugh . . .
Ecclesiastes 3:1,4 (RSV)

A mother's 17-year-old son came to her and said, 'Mum, the prom is next week and I'd really like to go, but I'm trying to save my earnings for more important things. You wouldn't consider giving me the money for the prom, would you?' His mother was a sucker for sentiment. The prom had been one of the highlights of her high school days, and wanting her son to enjoy this 'once in a lifetime' event as much as she had, she agreed. 'How much?' she asked.

Her son began enumerating the expenses: 'It's $70 for the tux rental, $10 for formal shoes, $15 for a corsage, $45 for dinner afterwards, $15 for a photo, $20 for my part of the limousine, $20 for the prom tickets, $20 for the chaperoned all-night party after the prom, $10 for breakfast the next morning . . . that's $225.' The mother gulped hard, but paid up.

As prom day approached, she asked her son, 'Who are you taking to the prom?' He said, 'I'm not going.' 'What?' the mother said. 'What about my money?' 'Well,' the son reasoned, 'I told you I was saving my money for something important. I said I'd *like* to go to the prom, but that's *way* too expensive. Some of the guys and I are going to a baseball game that night instead!'

In a perfect world . . .
children on trips
would say, 'Isn't
riding in the car fun!'
and then they'd
fall asleep.

A cheerful heart is a good medicine.
Proverbs 17:22 (RSV)

The Barton family was driving home in pouring rain one night. Mum and Dad were in the front seat and their two little girls in the back. Given the driving conditions and Mr Barton's need for concentration, conversation soon faded into silence and before long, the two girls fell asleep. After a hundred miles of motorway, they finally turned off for the last twenty miles of winding country road to their home.

Suddenly they were confronted by another car's blinding headlights. The car was coming over the crest of a hill, seemingly straight at them. It didn't slow . . . it didn't swerve . . . it didn't even seem to see them! Mr Barton was nearly blinded by the glare through his wet windshield. He swerved to avoid a crash and his tyres lost traction on the muddy shoulder. The car spun wildly in a circle, then skidded round. Finally Mr Barton regained control and the car came to a rest on the opposite side of the road, facing in the opposite direction they had been going.

As Mrs Barton caught her breath, her thoughts turned immediately to her children. She whirled round to see if they were still safely buckled into the back seat. As she did, the parents heard their five-year-old daughter complain, 'I was asleep, Daddy. Do it again!'

Fathers give daughters
away to other men
who aren't nearly good
enough . . .
so they can have
grandchildren that are
smarter than anybody's.

There is a right time for everything . . .
a time to laugh . . .
Ecclesiastes 3:1,4 (TLB)

Bill Cosby writes in *Fatherhood,* 'Some authority on parenting once said, "Hold them very close and then let them go." This is the hardest truth for a father to learn: that his children are continuously growing up and moving away from him (until, of course, they move back in). Such growth is especially bittersweet with a daughter because you are always in love with her.'

When rejection by a daughter occurs, Cosby advises, 'You have to remember that it means no lessening of her love. You must use this rejection to prepare yourself for others that will be coming, like the one I received on a certain day when I called my daughter at college. Someone in her dorm picked up the phone and I asked to speak to my daughter. The person left and returned about a minute later to say "She says she's sleeping right now."

'I was hurt to have my daughter put me on hold, but intellectually I knew that this was just another stage in her growth; and I remembered what Spencer Tracy had said in *Father of the Bride:* "Your son is your son till he takes him a wife, but your daughter is your daughter for all of your life." You are stuck with each other, and what a lovely adhesion it is.'

Other books in the
God's Little Devotional Series

God's Little Devotional Book for Couples
0 86347 272 9

God's Little Devotional Book for Everyday
0 86347 285 0

God's Little Devotional Book for Everyone
0 86347 234 6

God's Little Devotional Book for Kids
0 86347 286 9

God's Little Devotional Book for Mothers
0 86347 284 2

God's Little Devotional Book on Prayer
0 86347 235 4

God's Little Devotional Book for Teens
0 86347 325 3

God's Little Devotional Book for Women
0 86347 273 7